HOW TO GET INTO GRAD SCHOOL

HOW TO GET INTO GRAD SCHOOL

*Even If You're Broke, Dimwitted, or Spent Your Undergrad
Years so Smashed You Can't Even Spell GPA*

Revised Edition

JANICE HARPER, PH.D.

ISBN-13: 9780692730300
ISBN-10: 0692730303
Library of Congress Control Number: 2016909442
Back Door Press, Tacoma, Washington

TABLE OF CONTENTS

INTRODUCTION

(OR GRAD SCHOOLS AND HOW THEY GET THAT WAY)

If you are thinking about going to graduate school but aren't sure where to begin, if you think the cost is too prohibitive and you just can't afford it, or if you just have no idea what to study or what degree you should aim for, relax. I'm going to let you in on some open (and some not so open) secrets about how to get into graduate school—and get it paid for—including what to say and what not to say in the essay, how to get one or more faculty members to fight for your admission in the faculty meetings, how and where to find funding and employment in the university that will cover your tuition and living expenses, and how to work around the handicaps you fear might keep you from getting in—such as a low GPA, few references, or mediocre test scores.

I know. I've been there—as a grad student and a professor. When I made up my mind to go to grad school, I had everything working against me. I had a 2.7 GPA from a school I'd only attended for a year. Prior to that, I'd been jumping around the country from community colleges to state colleges for so long that by the time I finally did graduate, no one even knew me. Then I spent years jumping from job to job so that by the time I decided to go to grad school, I was thirty years old, which is to say, old meat.

To make matters worse, I was flat broke and didn't have any idea how to even apply to a grad school, much less what one really was. All I knew was that I wanted a Ph.D., and I wanted it in a field I had only ever taken one class in—and had earned a C minus. But not only did I get into grad school—and get it paid for—but by the time I graduated with that Ph.D. I had received over $100,000 in grants and fellowships, including a Fulbright award and a hefty grant from the National Science Foundation—even though I'd never scored above a C in any science class I'd ever taken.

I spent the next decade as a university professor where I taught graduate students. I evaluated grad school applications, sat in department meetings debating who to admit and who to reject and whose education we should pay for, taught graduate seminars, supervised graduate assistants, advised graduate students, supervised theses and dissertations, and helped students finishing their degrees get into other graduate programs where they could get more degrees. By the time I'd decided that the Ivory Towers were not where I wanted to spend my life, or they decided to hurl me out of the Towers for my uppity attitude, whichever story works, I knew the good, the bad and the ugly about not only the admissions process, but the whole charade of how to survive and succeed in graduate school and how and when to get out with the best chance of a decent job.

During my ten year career as a professor, I taught and mentored thousands of students, students who have gone on to careers as physicians, attorneys, government agents, authors, professors and no doubt more than a few prostitutes, drug dealers and thieves. And if there is anything I've learned from the time I decided I wanted to get into grad school to the time I got out altogether, it was this: it is not all that important how intelligent you are or how hard you work. Those things don't hurt, but *the real key to succeeding in grad school is knowing the rules of the game.* So I'm going to let you in on a few secrets about what it really takes to get into grad school, and you'll be surprised how easy it really is—and how easy it is for even the best student to get rejected, for no better reason than they didn't know the rules or what goes on inside those faculty meetings.

The first thing you need to understand before you even get started is exactly what a grad school is. A graduate school may mean to you a place to get an education and advance your career. That is all well and good, but to succeed, understand that from the perspective of those on the inside, a graduate school or program provides prestige to a university and ups their ranking, which in turn brings more donor money, more research grants, more students (and their tuition) and a bigger piece of the educational budgetary pie. It provides professors a pool of low-waged workers to teach their classes for them, grade their papers, do their research, write their peer-reviewed papers, and most importantly, feed their egos.

Some graduate schools actually teach useful skills, such as medical schools, law schools, even business administration programs. But even in these clinical or "applied" programs, the role of the graduate student is not so much to learn as it is to be enculturated into a specific professional culture where success depends upon social networks, communication skills and useful products—which is to say, papers, books, inventions, anything that can be commodified to promote someone else's profession. The more a graduate student succeeds in promoting the professions of those above him or her, the more beloved they will be by their professors and the department. Exploited, absolutely, but beloved—and hence supported—absolutely.

Now, before you write me off as overly cynical, let me be clear. There are as many good reasons to get a graduate degree as there are reasons not to. Getting a graduate degree over the course of a decade to enter a job market in massive debt where there are one hundred to four hundred applicants for every position and almost always requires relocating to another part of the country or the planet to be paid less than a dental assistant is not a good reason to get a graduate degree.

Gaining a better knowledge of one's profession and the credentials to be more competitive on the job market and/or get promoted, learning how to conduct research, think critically and write under pressure and in a manner which people will take seriously, or just delaying repaying the student loans (while not incurring any new ones) when you're unemployed and having an income in the meantime, are all good reasons to go to grad school—provided you get out quickly and with the most useful degree to help you achieve your professional dreams.

So, first thing, let's understand the different types of colleges and universities. (If you already know some of this stuff, bear with me; too many people simply don't.) Private schools are owned and controlled by private money—which means, rich people. They don't have to follow the same rules as the public schools, and that can help or hurt you depending on your situation (and if you play it right, you don't need to be rich to get in). Examples of private schools are liberal arts colleges which tend to have four-year terminal degrees, but often have graduate programs, usually at the Master's level.

Public colleges or universities receive funding from the state, so they are more controlled by certain rules. Whereas a private college can require that you swear to uphold a specific set of religious principles, for example, a public university cannot do that. But both private and public schools can set rules of admission, which may include a certain GPA, a certain GRE (Graduate Record Exam) score, and any other set of requirements. But the good news is, because they all want money, these rules are usually far more flexible than you might believe, particularly if you have a wealthy relative who is happy to donate lots of money. But most likely, you don't have such a relative—if you did, you'd probably already know the unwritten rules of getting into grad school.

Among public colleges, there are two main types: research institutes and teaching institutes. Almost all universities fancy themselves as research institutes, which means their primary purpose is to support the research of the faculty, obtain prestigious grant money, and produce notable scholarship, patents, and awards. If the school names begins with "University of" it is likely a research university. The same is true of any university ending in "State University." Almost always, the "University of" is considered superior to the "State University" (even though both are technically "state universities") but that does not mean that the reputation is deserved.

Within each university, the prestige and value of each department varies, so don't worry at this point about which type you should be aiming for. We'll get to that in a moment. For now, just understand that *a research institute wants and needs graduate students* to teach the undergrads, help the faculty do their research and get published, and maintain their department's prestige. The down-side is they have lots of graduate students, all competing for the same professors' attentions and the same graduate assistantships, and none of them are getting enough money or attention. But almost all of them are being overworked.

A teaching institute is a private college or university, or a state college or university (usually regional), that considers its primary mission to educate students. In these universities, there may well be graduate programs, and these programs may be desperate for students, but the faculty will teach most of the undergraduate classes and there won't be a big focus on faculty doing research and publishing. Faculty at teaching institutions will have heavy teaching loads and be under pressure to maintain excellent teaching reviews. Because faculty like graduate students to help them with their work, and because graduate students tend to look up to, if not sleep with, their professors, many faculty at teaching institutes will fight tooth and nail for devoted graduate students. They may be less likely to have any pots of money to pay these students, but they may be warm and welcoming to those they do have (and that means they still may find some money to support their favored grad students).

Within each school, there are different organizational levels that you will become familiar with. There is the Registrar's Office, which you probably remember from undergrad days. The Registrar's Office is in charge of your grades and degrees. You will need to contact the Registrar's Office of each school you went to as an undergrad, and have them send copies of your official transcripts to the schools you apply to. You can usually do that online, but we're getting ahead of ourselves here.

There is also the Admission's Office, which becomes less important in graduate school than it was in undergrad. *What is important in grad school is the Graduate School.* Each university will have a specific "Graduate School" which you can find on the university's website, and the Graduate School will list the requirements and procedures for admission—and for graduation. It will also often list valuable information about grants, funding opportunities, and even directions the grad school is going—which as I'll show you, can help you score some valuable points when you get to the letter of admission. (Graduate Schools also often fund graduate students directly, as I will explain.)

Keep in mind that for whatever school you decide to apply to, there will be the university's admission requirements, the graduate school's admission requirements, the department's admission requirements, and sometimes even a specific program within the department will have a different set of requirements. You will need to determine what each requires, and they usually always come down to these two criteria: Your GPA (undergraduate Grade Point Average); and your GRE (Graduate Record Exam) or other graduate exam scores (such as MCAT, Medical College Admissions Test, or LSAT, Law School Admissions).

In addition to these quantitative criteria, there are many unwritten, subjective qualities that the faculty look for and evaluate when deciding who to admit and who to reject, and figuring those out can make the difference between admission and rejection, no matter what your academic background.

Most schools require that applications—including GRE or other test scores—be submitted by December or January preceding Fall admission. This means that *it will take about one year from the time you get started on the application process, to the time you are admitted*. If you aren't sure what you will be doing in another year, but think you might want to go to graduate school, get started and get the application in. It doesn't mean you have to go if you are accepted, but it creates another opportunity for you if you are.

The Graduate Record Exam is required by most, but not all, schools (or the LSAT or MCAT or whatever entrance exam is required for your discipline). The GRE's are offered throughout the year and can be taken every thirty days for up to five times in a given year. Moreover, they are good for five years, so even if you decide not to go to graduate school the following year, they are still relevant for another five years. The GRE's test verbal, quantitative and analytical ability, and you are scored in each area separately. In some cases, there are separate subject areas that your discipline might require you test in, such as Biochemistry, Cell and Molecular Biology; Chemistry; Physics; Biology; Psychology; Mathematics; and English Literature. The subject tests are currently offered in September, October and April, so if you want to apply in one of these disciplines, keep these dates in mind.

If you do well on the GRE's, it can go far in offsetting a lousy GPA, and if you do well in both areas, outstanding! But if you blow it on the GRE's? Don't despair; some schools don't even require them. I'll say a bit more on that topic further on, but for now, let's get started on getting you into grad school.

Chapter 1

● ● ●

CHOOSE YOUR DEGREE WISELY

You may already know what degree you want—a Ph.D., M.A., MBA, JD, MD or something else altogether. But sometimes, other degrees get you out faster and you end up more employable in the same field than if you'd gotten the degree you really wanted, or combining degrees can make you more employable with little extra effort, or help you to overcome a lousy GPA. Let me explain.

When I decided I wanted a Ph.D., I knew I could never get into a decent program with my lousy GPA and no recent academic contacts. So I chose a regional school in my home state where the requirements for admission were much lower. I was able to not only get into a grad program because not many people were applying for admission there, but one year later when I began to apply for Ph.D. programs, I had a 4.0 GPA, had written specific papers in my field, and had professors who would write letter of recommendation for me. It still wouldn't get me into Harvard (though had I known a few tricks back then, that, too, might have been achievable), but it got me into one of the nation's leading programs in my field.

What I didn't know then was that once you get into a Ph.D. program, you will have to do that M.A. all over again. Once I finished my M.A. at the regional school and moved to the big state university for the doctoral program, I discovered that only one course could be waived. If I had done my

M.A. in a different, but related field, I would have still been able to get at least one course waived, but I would have graduated with degrees in two different fields—thereby enhancing my future employability. More importantly, had I obtained that intermediate graduate degree in a "clinical" or "applied" field, it probably would have made me more employable, and at a higher salary, than the Ph.D. did. What are some examples of this type of degree combination?

A Master's of Social Work (MSW) combined with a Ph.D. in psychology is in many ways more useful than an M.A. and Ph.D. in psychology, and takes no additional time or money. Want to get a Ph.D. in political science? It's a good degree. But a 3 year JD first might make more sense than a 2 year M.A. in poli-sci (though it will indeed be pricier; but you could well make that up through the increased income you would earn). Interested in forensic science? The job market is shrinking in that one, but no forensic program is likely to tell you they are admitting far more graduate students than the job market can absorb. So you might be better off if you combine a Master's in Criminal Justice with a Ph.D. in a broader field, such as chemistry. You can add electives in forensics along the way and end up just as employable, if not more so, than had you graduated with a Ph.D. in forensics.

Do you want to be a writer but want to be employable as well? Sadly, publishing has changed drastically in recent years, and if you want to survive economically, instead of an M.A. or MFA (Master's in Fine Arts) in English, you may be better off getting a graduate degree in marketing and social media, while taking some writing classes on the side. You want to travel the world and live with exotic tribes? The days of Margaret Mead are over, but an M.A. in medical anthropology followed by an MD often takes less time than a Ph.D. in medical anthropology and is far more marketable. Or a Master's in Public Health (MPH) with a Ph.D. in anthropology may be the way to go—the MPH will likely get you the job, not the Ph.D., but at least people will call you doctor.

So if you are considering a Ph.D., ask yourself what clinical or applied degrees—degrees that will allow you to go into practice for yourself, solicit clients, get a job right away—you can pursue first. It will not necessarily take you any more time or money (sometimes it will take more money, but that's usually in programs like law or medicine where you can actually find work), but it can really make a huge difference in your employability, and in many cases will get you out of school much faster.

If, however, you only want a Master's degree, unless it is a clinical or applied degree (as in, nursing, MSW [Masters in Social Work], M.Ed. [Masters in Education], MPH [Masters in Public Health], MBA [Masters in Business Administration] or something similar), you are probably wasting your time. There is very little you can learn in two years of graduate school that you can't learn on your own, faculty will be more interested in their doctoral students than the terminal Master's students, and the degree is not likely to get you a job at the local mall, much less making any real money. Moreover, funding rarely goes to terminal master's degree candidates when there are doctoral programs. So if you want only a two to three year degree, that's perfectly reasonable, but just *be sure it's one that will give you a professional credential you can really use*—such as certification to go into practice for yourself or obtain a job in a decent job market.

A word of caution here: many departments, particularly ones that confer degrees in the humanities and social sciences, try to recruit students by creating "certificate programs" or "applied certificate programs" or some such thing because they know students are catching on that advanced degrees in these fields are pretty useless. I have designed many of these "cutting edge" certificate programs and sat in on meetings with university administrators extolling their virtues—which are always, always, about bringing in tuition dollars, preferably the big bucks (anything prefaced with "professional" is usually designed for corporations to pay the inflated tuition costs; get those only if your corporation will pay you to go to school and hence avoid the workplace).

I've been one of the biggest pushers of these certificates to administrators because they love them, but I would never advise a student to pay a penny for them. Faculty rarely care about them, they are designed to look good on paper but provide little real worth, they very often fade into obscurity within a couple of years, they are almost always relatively new and thus, untested, and nobody outside the university knows what they hell they are. Unless you are a faculty member trying to impress the dean with your marketing acumen, steer clear of "certificate" programs that are not well recognized in your field. (Teaching certificates, various health professional certificates conferring an expertise, and that sort of thing are different beasts altogether; they have been around awhile or are new twists on well established programs that grant useful professional credentials.)

Finally, Hollywood and television have inspired countless people to pursue various careers that look glamorous from afar, and often those people have gone on to be quite successful and happy in those careers once they got there. But as the population has increased and the media have saturated our lives 24-hours a day, the number of people applying to grad school because they have been inspired by fiction on the big screen has only served academic departments that get more grad students and hence more money. Any career made popular by fiction inevitably leads to a surplus of disillusioned graduates who don't stand a snowball's chance in hell of finding work in the career they thought they were getting into. Don't be that graduate.

Want to go into forensics because you love CSI? You'll join tens of thousands of others (curiously, mostly women), who are headed for a rude awakening, lots of science classes (not that there's anything wrong with that), and a job market saturated with far more job seekers than dead bodies. If forensics is your dream, head for a grad school in the sciences, minor in criminalistics, and be prepared to work in a lab solving a variety of puzzles, only some of which may be related to crime. You may well end up working exclusively in forensics, but chances are that in order to get there, you will need to master your craft peering through microscopes for some multi-national corporation, not traipsing through crime scenes to find out who dunnit and how they dunnit.

Then again, if you really want to solve crimes you could go to medical school and become a medical examiner in a major urban area, and you'll have no end of murder victims to keep you entertained. Or go to law school, work a couple of years for a public defender and/or prosecutor's office, and specialize in criminal law. Throw in some theater classes (really; just ask famed attorney Jerry Spence who runs a theater camp for lawyers) and gain some experience in investigation (check out the university's School of Journalism, though they rarely teach investigative journalism these days), work in claims for an insurance company, take courses in police procedure and/or volunteer as an investigative intern for the public defender's office or a local criminal attorney, and you may end up spending your life solving or covering up all sorts of grizzly crimes. Just don't join the legions of CSI fans who have no idea what a career in forensics actually entails.

In other words, what you see on TV or the big screen rarely corresponds to real life. And faculty recognize in a heartbeat the applicant who has been inspired by make believe. Remember, graduate school is expensive and time consuming. Make a realistic decision about what you want to do with your life, and chart a sensible course to get there—one which will produce the best employment options once you graduate. Have dreams and pursue them, but do so with awareness and insight and you're more likely to reach them.

Chapter 2

● ● ●

LINE UP YOUR SCHOOLS

By this point you've given some thought to what kind of degree you want. But do you know which schools you should apply to? Apply to as many as you can (though remember, it costs to apply to each school, so be strategic). A good idea is to start locally. Tuition is cheapest in public schools in your home state (but if you get funded, out of state tuition is usually waived), though it makes no difference with private schools—it's expensive for everyone.

If you have a low GPA, look at regional schools—these are the ones that have Northern, Southern, Western, Eastern somewhere between the words "university" and whatever state they are in. Don't feel discouraged if you really want to get into the very best school. Regional schools can be very good places to get a Master's degree. You don't have to spend your life there, they're the perfect stepping stone to bigger leagues, and many of them are very decent with excellent faculty. A good regional school is far better than a mediocre top tier school, especially if you get decent, supportive faculty (which you very often don't find at the more prestigious schools, especially if you aren't in a doctoral program).

Can you relocate? If you can, you should begin looking at schools that offer the best program in your area of interest. You should look at, but probably ignore, things like the U.S. News and World Report College Rankings (www.usnews.com/rankings); they have very subjective criteria for basing their evaluations, so think of those rankings as useful information, not necessarily facts. What is really more useful to you is an understanding of the reputation and strengths of specific departments, rather than the universities themselves (unless you get into the Ivy Leagues, in which case, who cares, just survive it).

You can look at the professional organizations and associations for your chosen discipline, and a perusal of their websites will often list the best programs, though even those are usually out of date. But at least give it a look, and try just Googling, "best graduate programs in hocus pocus" and see what comes up—but remember, a department can offer the very best program in cutting edge hocus pocus for twenty years, then with a couple of retirements and a few new hires, that program is dying a slow death while others throughout the nation are springing up (but they won't want you to know that). You will find out the best programs with some Googling, some website perusal, and a few calls or visits to professors or professionals in your preferred field of study. Talk to anyone you know who might know where the best programs are and see which names you find popping up most often.

Now, here's an important point that you may not realize: *most universities, particularly the "research institutes" don't like to admit their own graduates to their Ph.D. programs.* So if you pretty much only have the option of going to your local university or none at all because you can't relocate just now, and you already have your undergrad from there, you have a potential obstacle. If that's the case, applying to a different discipline than the one you have your undergrad degree in may be all you need to do to avoid rejection. And if you still want to stick with the same discipline at the same university you did your undergrad at, okay, there's still a way around it in most cases. Talk to the professors you know, or if you don't know any because you never spoke to any and all your classes were taught by grad students, then just contact someone (whom, exactly, we'll get to in the next section).

But if your plan is to get into a leading Ph.D. program at a specific school, and you can't get into that program directly so you figure you will get your M.A. there to get a foot in the door, and then you will apply to the Ph.D. program, *watch out!* While that does work sometimes, many faculty are dead set against allowing their own Master's students into their Ph.D. programs. Get your Master's elsewhere, then apply to their Ph.D. program.

In these departments, no matter how excellent a student may be, the faculty often vote against admission. Why? Because theoretically, the best students have well-rounded educations from diverse institutions. But really? The real reason some faculty really don't like it is because they consider themselves so stellar that to admit their own students is like taking the dregs off the street—they want to pretend the most competitive students in the nation are knocking down their doors—while the graduates they turn out are recruited across the nation (or else they must not be so good and hence, should be rejected). And then there are the rankings. The more of their own graduates they admit to their doctoral program, the lower their rankings among the rankers. The faculty will bitch and moan about the worthlessness of those rankings (unless they're ranked among the top), but they don't want to do anything that would lower those rankings either, so they may be very cautious about admitting their own undergraduates to their graduate programs.

It's rubbish, but it's rubbish that won't go away. I have seen excellent students with high GPA's who worked their asses off for their professors only to be refused entry into Ph.D. programs because they had families or well-paying jobs and couldn't relocate and therefore were considered "locals" and less valued. It's that petty. So don't plan for "getting a foot in the door," of a prestigious Ph.D. program by first getting your Master's there. If you really want to get into that program, first see what their policy—and their practice—is about accepting their own students into their doctoral program, and if it's not good, then either consider scratching them off your list altogether because they're too self-absorbed and short-sighted to be worth your time, or get your Master's elsewhere, while cultivating your relationships with the faculty at the doctoral school of your dreams.

Chapter 3

● ● ●

THINK TWICE ABOUT ONLINE DEGREES

It's increasingly common for people who are working fulltime, busy with families, or unable to get into a traditional university department, to pursue online graduate programs. For the most part, online degrees are a bad idea. They are not well respected in academia nor by many employers, and for good reason. They are generally not too picky about who they admit, there is no real way to tell if the person taking the exams and participating in the online discussions is the student who enrolled (or someone the student has paid to do the work), the faculty are paid so low that they are typically not the cream of the crop and often have only a Master's degree themselves, the degrees can be extremely expensive, and the classroom experience and faculty interactions are significantly less interactive and meaningful than what you would find in a real university. When potential employers are looking for someone with an advanced degree, the applicant with the online degree will not impress. So an online degree is best considered a last option. But what happens if you're down to your last option? You find the best possible one.

The best online graduate degrees are the ones that come from "real" universities or colleges. By that I mean state or private universities that in recent years have added online graduate degrees as options for "remote" students, not universities or colleges that were established for the primary purpose of offering online degrees. In the former, experienced faculty with doctorates are more likely to be your professors—they're teaching the online class probably for some extra money, but perhaps also because they enjoy the teaching experience and want to do it. In that case, they are likely to be quite creative and enthusiastic. In any case, they're experienced faculty with an expertise in what they are teaching—not recent graduates with no real expertise in their field beyond what they themselves learned in college.

Yet even when from reputable universities, online degrees are stigmatized. They also keep you apart from the faculty and students, no matter how interactive you might be online. The students that the faculty interact with on a daily basis in real life and real time are the students who get the most attention—and the relationships that are established in that atmosphere are more lasting and meaningful than most online relationships. So if it comes down to choice, choose the real life degree over the virtual one.

But if you must choose the online degree, choosing a brick and mortar university for that online degree is a smarter move because in most cases, you can conceal the fact that it was an online degree. Your degree will come from the University of Scientific Achievement, not Online U. You're less likely to be weeded out on the job market, and if it does come out that it was an online degree, you can just say you took the classes remotely for financial or logistical reasons, but they were taught by tenured faculty at the university. *An online degree from an established university that offers the remote classes as a supplement to its traditional offerings does not have the same stigma as the universities that only offer (or prioritize) online degrees or have limited classroom options.*

There is another online option that may be suitable for some people and that is the online executive degree. Executive degrees are similar to the "professional certificate" tracts I discussed (and trashed) earlier. But unlike the professional certificate tracts, there are many graduate programs from reputable and even Ivy League schools that are taught by excellent faculty and result in graduate degrees (not "certificates") that are well respected by employers. These degrees are typically MBA programs, but they also include other professional programs in leadership, health administration, and similar fields and are marketed to people who have several years of professional experience and are currently working fulltime in their field. If that sounds like you, you might find that an online executive graduate degree from a reputable school is just the ticket—and might even be paid for by your employer. But be prepared—one of the reasons they are respected is that they are often selective about who they admit. Unlike the online mills, they won't admit just anyone. You still have to do your homework before they'll let you in.

Chapter 4

● ● ●

FIND THE BEST DEPARTMENTS

Once you've decided on schools that interest you, take a close look at the departments (though this often happens in the reverse order; often you will find the best departments in your desired field of study, then you will want to look at the school after looking at the department). *Spend some time looking at the department website to see who the faculty are.* "Faculty Emeritus" means they are retired. They may still be lurking around, but they are the ghosts of the department. Don't focus on them; they rarely concern themselves with graduate students, particularly at the pre-admissions stage. (There is an exception, however. If they are experts in the field you wish to study, and other faculty have less expertise in that area, the emeritus professor may be the first person you want to speak to.) Here's what you need to know about faculty and status.

Professors have the most status, but not necessarily the most influence. When did they get their degree? How much, how often, and how recently have they been publishing? What are they teaching? Do they have websites? Take a look at them. If you see a professor with a mid-century Ph.D. who wrote a classic book in his or her field but there is no evidence that they have published anything in the last five years and they don't have a website or other sign of being current, chances are, you're dealing with an old goat who may well be connected, but is on his or her last legs before being put out to Emeritus pasture. But old goat doesn't mean dead goat, and there are a couple of reasons why you may well want to get to know an old goat or two. First, they may be brighter than the whole lot of them, but just a bit more cynical or tired. Second, they may be lonely and very much anxious to work with an eager grad student. And third, they are usually well connected in the institution.

If, on the other hand, you find a full professor who has a website, publishes every sentence they spit out, attends tons of conferences and has a whole list of grad students they've mentored, advised, supervised and promoted, they are worth contacting, *but not counting on.* They are probably way too busy and overwhelmed with the demands of grad students to really want any more. And they may well be very encouraging initially, but completely forget who you are by the time you finally arrive. It's always a good idea to contact them and get them on your side, but don't count on them as being your mentor or your only contact in the department. You'll want others on your side, and we'll get to how you can do that in the next section.

Associate Professors are tenured but scrambling for that next promotion. They share many of the similar characteristics of full professors, but are often far more arrogant than their seniors (but not always; never assume anything of anyone before you actually meet them). Associate Professors do have tenure, so they have important influence, but they may or may not be well liked, and they may or may not like you. Just know that they are tenured, and still working their way up the ladder.

Assistant Professors have no job security and are scrambling for tenure. They may be way too busy for grad students but are expected to be recruiting them nonetheless. They may have zero influence in the department, they may be on their way out the door, or they may be considered "the future of the department" and be very influential. It's certainly a good idea to get an Assistant Professor on your side (as well as one or two above them) because they are likely to be eager to mentor incoming grad students.

Instructors have very little influence and a great deal of work. They are the ones who are likely to be supervising graduate students at large universities, so they are definitely people to respect (all the more so because they are paid next to nothing for working from sun up to sun down). You probably won't be contacting any of them before you apply, unless they specialize in your area of interest, but once you get there, befriend them. They may well become your bosses if you end up as a teaching assistant (which is the most common source of financial aid).

Adjunct Professors are usually people who teach in other departments or universities or work outside the university altogether. Sometimes they are very well known in their discipline, and usually they know something about the scuttlebutt of the department, but as a rule they have little or no influence, they rarely take graduate students because they have no money to pay them (and usually receive no pay from the university), and tend to be fairly distant from the department. But if they specialize in something that interests you, it's certainly worth contacting them to see what you can find out about their work and the department. They may also end up on your graduate committee should you ask them, and thus have influence over how quickly and painlessly you graduate.

What you want to look for is a department with a balance of Assistant, Associate and full Professors. *A department with few or no Associate Professors is usually a bad sign*—it means they are top heavy, with a whole bunch of new-comers (the Assistant Professors) who are probably changing things (with considerable resistance). With few Associate Professors, there is usually a marked division within the department and tensions are high. Worse, when it comes to putting together your graduate committee, you may find that there are few people with tenure you can put on it, and those who do have it may be retiring before you graduate.

Another thing you want to look for is that there are faculty working and teaching in the area that interests you. As a general rule, if there are two to three faculty working in or near your area in some way, then it is a good sign that this is a department to consider. Any less and you may have some very real problems because hardly anyone will know anything about what it is you're studying (and the lone faculty who does may well be an odd duck as well). Possibly worse, if there is only one professor in your area of study, you will work with that professor whether or not you want to.

Even if you are thrilled to work with them, if they don't want to work with you, you'll end up worse off than if the department had no one in your area. Instead, you're likely to have someone rejecting you from the onset, someone who specializes in your field who doesn't think you're worth their time or attention. If they have to work with you when they'd really rather not, they will not be likely to support or encourage you and will probably give preference to other graduate students. Even if you love each other, if they do leave—from death, retirement, illness, termination or moving on to another university—you could find yourself a few years into your studies with no one to supervise you—or strongly recommend you to employers—at the end of your graduate studies.

You also want to be sure that the department does not religiously adhere to a specific theoretical model and resent anyone with differing ideas—which is very common, and often difficult to figure out until you get there. Just because their website celebrates "diversity," doesn't make it so—particularly when it comes to ideological diversity.

To get a sense of how open the department is to a range of theoretical approaches, take a look at what the different faculty are publishing and teaching. Are there any particular theories that pop up repeatedly? Are all the faculty interested in the same thing? Each faculty member should have their CV (Curriculum Vita) available through their website (with the emphasis on "should," very often they don't). Read over what they teach and publish to get a sense of whether or not different perspectives are represented in the department.

Another thing to look for is cooperation. Are faculty publishing co-authored articles (with each other and with their graduate students)? Be aware, however, that in the STEM fields, as well as most health fields, faculty are expected to put each other's names on just about everything they publish, so it is not uncommon to see articles with a dozen or more "authors." In the social sciences and humanities, however, single authored publications are the norm which means that co-authored articles may be a sign of cooperative writing efforts.

A good sign of a cooperative department is that faculty publish, teach or run programs together; a bad sign is that only two faculty publish or teach together and do so all the time. The first means there is a spirit of cooperation, the second is a red flag that there is a faction that probably always votes and gossips together and everyone else resents them.

All departments have their divisions, and sometimes these divisions are no big deal, while other times they are battle lines marking raging internecine wars. Do you see the full Professors publishing articles in one theoretical or topical area, while the Assistant Professors and younger Associates publish in another? That may be a sign that faculty resent each other and don't work well together or at the very least, that the old guard is on the way out and things are changing.

On the other hand, are faculty publishing or working on programs together across sub-disciplinary and theoretical lines? Are senior faculty publishing and working with junior faculty? If so, that is a good sign. *Remember, no department is perfect, none are even close to it, and inter-departmental battles always rage. But many departments are especially toxic, and you want to avoid those departments if you can.*

A helpful way to identify a toxic department is to go to the *Chronicle of Higher Education*, (http://www.chronicle.com) and *Inside Higher Education* (http://www.insidehighered.com) and see if there have been any articles on the department (or university) about lawsuits, bitter tenure denials, major reorganization of departments (such as merging departments, a sure sign there will be tension) or other signs that the department may be toxic. If you need an account to access the articles in these sites (you won't need it just to do the search), check if your local library has access to the publications, or call a university library, say you are Dr. So and So (use your own name, no one will look it up), and you're working from home and for some reason you can't access the department's library site from your computer. Say you need to look up an article that you read in one of these publications and can't remember which one it was in. Ask if they can tell you the university's password to access it. It will probably work.

If it doesn't, and even if it does, Google the name of the department you are interested in, and read the first ten or so pages of the search results to see if anything really ugly comes up. If it does, consider it a red flag, no matter what you might later be told of the matter (it will be cleansed and revised as time goes on to make the department and existing faculty appear picture perfect). Departments with only one gender or race represented are a red flag, and departments with lots of new faculty and lots of faculty "on leave" or which have been recently reorganized into new departments, are usually fraught with problems.

Remember, just about every department has its ghosts and demons, but the more aware you are of red flags, the more likely you can avoid the most toxic departments (or at least the most toxic faculty).

Another important consideration is whether there are enough course offerings in the area you want to study. If there are few course offerings that would interest you or relate to what you are studying, don't rely on anyone's promises that they will be added. Be sure there are enough courses for you to take to make it worth your while. Also be sure those courses are actually taught. University and/or departmental websites usually list not just the courses offered, but they should have a tab for "current students." Click on that and look up the upcoming courses available for enrollment. They usually include two semesters, which can give you an idea of what is currently offered. You may not be able to access the catalog without a password, but usually you can.

Once you have a sense of the courses that are offered, or said to be offered, that are of interest to you, write them down. When you contact the department, and you will, and/or faculty, which you will, you will want to ask if those courses will be offered in the near future. Quite often you'll find the course listings way out of date, but either way, knowing what specific courses are offered in your area will help you make a wise decision about which school or schools to aim for, and which are a waste of your time.

Then, once you've found the departments that interest you, take another, closer look, at the university. *Your purpose here is no longer to see if it's the best fit for you, but to figure out how to pitch yourself as the best fit for them.*

Chapter 5

● ● ●

GET TO KNOW THE UNIVERSITY A LITTLE BIT MORE

Now that you have an idea of where you want to apply, go to the website of each university and look at the university's "Mission Statement." It's usually found somewhere in "about the school" section or if not easily found, just type it into the site's search engine. It will say things about knowledge and critical thinking and their commitment to diversity and preparing students for the future and a bunch of high-sounding nonsense. After you've read a few you'll see they all pretty much say the same thing. In reality, mission statements aren't something people really pay all that much attention to and rarely does a university or any institution want real critical thinking or diversity of ideas; they really want conformity and unwavering acceptance of whatever higher administration is up to.

Mission statements are pretty much just written for the funders and donors to show the institution is on the cutting edge of whatever nonsense is the latest nonsense. (Not that commitment to diversity or critical thinking are nonsense; it's the failure of most in higher administration to really mean it when you come right down to it that is so nonsensical.)

So if the mission statement is nonsense, why should you read it? Because it will contain "useful buzzwords." Make a note of any that stand out, such as "applied research" (which means research that has some use to the world), community outreach, and more importantly, whatever their new "strengths" or "commitments" are. This is where they'll bring attention to whatever they have just sunk a bunch of money into. You can use this information to help decide which school or department to apply to within the university, or maybe how to craft your letter to make it sound like what you want to study in any given department is related to that focus. When we discuss writing the admissions essay, we'll get back to this point, but for now, just start familiarizing yourself with the website.

Within each university there are a number of "schools" and "colleges" which house the departments. Here's where you might get confused between universities and colleges. Within universities, there are a number of "colleges," but a small college, such as a liberal arts college, will likely have only departments, and possibly "schools."

Assuming you're looking at a university website, you'll note that there will be schools of natural sciences, agricultural sciences, social sciences, humanities, business, health and allied fields, that sort of thing. See what departments are in the college where your favored department is housed and take a look at their faculty. If you're looking at a liberal arts college, then focus on the departments and schools.

Make a note of any programs or faculty you see in other departments that might overlap with your interests. Then take a look at the college's Mission Statement, to give yourself an idea of the direction they are going in; it will pretty much mimic the university's mission statement, but pay attention to any subtle differences. They may or may not be meaningful; the more aware you are of the college and university missions, however, the better prepared you are to fit into it, and to start learning to speak their language.

Then do this bit of magic: go to the search engine for the college's site and type in "meeting minutes" in quotes. You will also want to go back and search meeting minutes for the university itself, but for now, just try it in the schools or colleges where the departments that interest you are housed (and later be sure to do it for the departments you will apply to). Half the time, nothing will come up. But the other half of the time, you will hit pay dirt. Many departments, colleges and institutes in universities (and many workplaces, it's a useful trick all around) routinely put their meeting minutes up on the internet. They may not be marked for the public to find, but if you put the term in the search engine, they often come up because the administrative assistant responsible for posting them didn't realize they were accessible. If you do find them, they will contain information on budget cuts, grad admissions, future hiring plans, and programs that are being cut or built up. This is "inside information" that you can use when you speak to faculty and craft your letter (not letting on, of course, that you read the meeting minutes! You want to sound as if you just naturally fit in).

Similarly, type in "strategic plan" and see what's up ahead. This will tell you where they are investing money, and where they are cutting programs, all information that will help you in deciding first, if this is the right place for you and second, what kinds of seeds to plant in your application, such as what you would like to study. If you don't find a strategic plan in the department's site, go to the university's main site and type it in. They'll have one. (This is a good idea for any organization you are applying to for employment, so keep it in mind.)

Then you want to take a look at the institutes and centers. *Every university, and particularly research institutions, have a number of interdisciplinary centers and institutes which provide faculty and graduate students with funding and publishing opportunities, as well as opportunities for networking.* Look at the university websites and you will see that there will be some sort of page that lists them. Then take a look at any that could in any way be related to what you want to study. Make a note of their faculty, their director, and any indication that they have either a) funding available or b) graduate students working there (just take a look at who works there; most employ grad students).

Now that you have done all this background research, there are few more things to do: check online for the student newspaper and local newspaper and see what they've written about the university and department over the last couple of years to get a sense of how satisfied faculty and students are. You'll often find stories to make your hair stand on end, but hopefully, you won't. And if you do, be sure to check the date of any such articles or postings. Is this an old story from a decade ago? Chances are, things have changed. (Well, no, chances are nothing's changed, but that particular issue is in the past.) Is it one disgruntled commenter or a whole slew of them? Are faculty publicizing their frustrations? If so, that's a bad sign. At any rate, see what's out there, and don't believe everything you read. But do file it under, "useful information."

If there are any graduate student associations in the department, see if they have a website, webpage, newsletter or other resource available. You can always contact some of the graduate students listed on these web sites, but the chances of running into a disgruntled student are high, and you might find yourself getting really poor advice and information. On the other hand, you may get very helpful information, decent advice, and make a welcoming new friend. Just be judicious, and realize one person's opinion is just one source of information.

Alright, so now that you've done all this reconnaissance, you're ready to get started contacting faculty.

Chapter 6

●   ●   ●

GET A PROFESSOR (OR TWO) ON YOUR SIDE

Here's how admissions are usually decided. The applications come in, and they pile up in the Administrative Assistant's office. Faculty may or may not get to peruse them as they sit there, but eventually, they are circulated to the faculty to review and/or comment on. After that they may go to a department graduate school committee, which is typically three to five faculty who will meet to discuss which applications to put on the short list. Then there will be one to several rounds of meetings of the full faculty in the department who will discuss, if not fight over, who to admit and who to fund.

As a general rule, the first thing faculty are going to be looking for is anyone interested in what interests them. The second thing they are going to notice is if any of the applicants' names are familiar. And they will also be looking at what undergraduate school you went to. If it's an Ivy League school, kudos! They'll like that. If it's not, don't worry, you still stand a shot.

After that, it's who wrote the reference letters, and the GPA and the GRE scores. Then they'll get to your essay, which is where almost everyone blows it. So here is where you want all the faculty to notice how well written, thoughtful, and cutting edge your essay is. And you want them all to think, 'I'd really like to work with this student' or 'That student would be a great fit in our department.' If your scores and GPA are high and/or your letters of reference stellar, you want them to notice that, as well. If not, you want them to give as little weight to those weaknesses as possible and notice other qualities you have that will suggest you'll do well and be an interesting student to have around.

There may be someone listed on the department website as the Chair of the Graduate Admissions Committee. If so, that person is someone you should contact for your initial round of questions. But these positions typically rotate, so what you see on the website might be last year's Chair. If so, they will either let you know who you should contact, or they will ignore you. If they ignore you (as in, no answer for a week or more), just call the department and ask who is chairing the graduate committee. If there is a person who has been appointed to chair the graduate admissions committee, then that is the person you will ask about procedures. They may or may not have much influence, but chances are they'll play a key role in who makes the first cut, so get in touch with them and be sure they know who you are.

You also want two to three faculty, or even just one if that's all you've got, to see your name, know who you are, and want you in the department. That is the person who is going to defend any weaknesses when they are raised (and they will be) and that is the person who is going to be most likely to help get you funded so that you don't have to pay any tuition and hopefully earn an income while you get your degree. So you want to be sure that you have such a person or people on your side, and you want to be sure that they aren't psychotic cut-throats who will eventually sabotage you, sadists who will work you to death for their own benefit, or lunatics who will drag you down along with them. It's not always easy to know, however, but I get to that later on.

Once you've found the faculty in the department and seen what their interests are, take a look at their Curriculum Vita, which should be on the website. Google them so you know what they've been up to. *And then—and this is very important—take a look at their work!* You don't have to read it all; in fact, you don't have to read any of it in its entirety. But by reading the abstracts (the summary at the beginning of every peer-reviewed article) and the introductions and conclusions, you have a pretty good idea of what they're doing. Take a look at their bibliographies—who do they cite the most in their articles and books? Be sure you at least scan the articles or books to be sure they aren't citing someone a lot because they've devoted their careers to slashing their work to pieces. Your aim is to know which scholars they most admire and which they do not. Knowing who influences them will go a long way not just by impressing them, but in helping to determine if they'd be the right professor for you. You might both love studying how the earth was formed, but if they believe the earth is flat and you're convinced it's not, you might have a problem.

The point is, whatever their specialty, faculty have their own way of looking at it, their own theoretical bent. Be sure you understand it at least sufficiently to know if you're on the same page.

The next question you want to ask is where did they get their degrees? Any faculty who graduated from the same undergraduate college or university you went to is probably worth contacting. Most people take pride in their alma mater and will show an extra bit of interest in those who went to the same school.

What kinds of grants do they get? If you're pursuing a doctorate, you want to align with the faculty who know how to bring in money. They may have funding to support you, and they may be able to teach a course or supervise an independent study in grant writing. What do they teach? (If it isn't clearly indicated on the department website, look up the course schedules and see what they are teaching.) If the classes they teach align with your interests, be sure to contact them.

If they are "on leave" then that might mean they may not be returning. If they're on leave for fieldwork or parental leave, they'll probably be back. If they're on leave because they're being tried for homicide or the department is taking up a collection to pay for their cancer treatment, then it's more iffy. A general rule of thumb is if they're on leave for a visiting teaching position or pending university inquiry into alleged misconduct, they're probably on the job market.

How do you find out? Look up their CV and their departmental website to see if they've updated it to include a visiting appointment or field research somewhere. Google their name and you might find some news reports of any investigations, or you may find an announcement at another university that they will be guest faculty for the coming year. If that doesn't work, call the department and ask the Administrative Assistant when they will be returning; tell her or him that you are thinking of applying, and wondered if the professor on leave will be there in the coming future. What they say won't necessarily tell you as much as how they say it—do they sound confident that the faculty member is returning? As in, "Dr. Dedicated is doing research but yes, he'll be back in the spring," or "Professor Productive is on maternity leave, but she can't wait to get back!" But if you hear, "Uh," pause, "I'm sure she'll be back at least next year," or a snide, "We aren't sure," with the tone of a bitter ex-wife, you can pretty much bet they are on the job market and best not to be contacted unless you really want to work with them. In that case, be confident they are still checking their emails and feel free to contact them.

Only after you have a good idea of what the faculty member has published and teaches and is currently working on, however, should you contact them. If you contact a faculty member and show little or no awareness of what they have written, they will see you as sucking up and just hoping for their help. They still might offer it, if they really need to recruit grad students (and most Assistant Professors do). But they won't exactly be seduced.

But if you show that you have read what they wrote, recognize their reputation, and want to work with them, then they will listen. I once wrote to a professor telling him that even though I didn't agree at all with his conclusions, I considered him the best versed in the area I wanted to study and wanted to study with him. He was delighted to work with me, and we laughed often about his efforts to convert me and my efforts to resist. Now I don't really recommend this strategy, I've since discovered that most professors are so narcissistic that they'd never get over being offended, but the important thing was, I meant it. I had read almost everything this professor had ever written, and I was honored to work with him, even if I didn't share his conclusions. By the time he retired, I'd realized he was probably more insightful than I was, and he remains the best professor I ever had.

When you do contact them, send a brief email, introducing yourself. *Address them as "Professor" or "Dr." but never by their first name.* You'd be surprised how many potential students contact professors by addressing them by their first name, or Mr., Mrs., or Ms. (women faculty are far more likely to be addressed in this manner). It instantly marks you as unprofessional and insulting. Use Dr. or Professor. If they want to be called by their first name (and some do), they'll let you know.

Explain your interest in applying to the program, and ask if you can call or meet them to discuss the program. Tell them what you have read of theirs, but don't go overboard with the schmoozing. That will work against you every time. Just be honest, and show an interest in their work, and an interest in working with them in some capacity. Now here's where you need to be careful. Some faculty will totally ignore you, but most won't. Some will pretty much brush you off with a general hello, reference to the program and tell you to send in your application. And some—the most promising—will be friendly, will ask about your background and ambitions, and will be happy to talk with you. Those are the faculty who are most likely to help you.

Some, however, will take their interest in you even further—they'll consider you their property, and decide that you will work with them, they will be your advisor, and you will write a thesis or dissertation that they will supervise. And that might be exactly what you want. *But no matter how much you want to work with them, no matter how impressed you are with their work, you will not know if you want to work with them—and they with you—until you have been there for at least a semester.*

So give yourself some wiggle room; *whoever you work with is going to have considerable power over your career, so don't head to the alter until you've had a taste of the ever after.* Let them know you are also contacting this or that other faculty in the department—but don't gush about these other colleagues; just show respect. This will signal 1) you are professional; 2) you recognize that other faculty may be just as likely to be your advisor; and 3) you are being selective.

Keep in mind whenever you interact with a faculty member, *you don't know what they think of their colleagues.* Eventually, you will, because faculty are notorious for gossiping with grad students and trashing their colleagues, but they may consider another faculty member you're communicating with to be a quack, a rival, a has-been, or a real gem. So be diplomatic. *(And don't fall for the bait if they ask how an interview or email exchange went with a colleague or anything else that smacks of getting you to take sides. If that happens, proceed with caution if not run the other way.)*

If a faculty member sends you anything, such as an article they have writ-ten, or something someone else in your field of mutual interest has written, read it ASAP. And then thank them for sharing the article with you, and letting them know what you thought of it.

Don't babble in the email, keep it succinct, but *end by asking if you could meet with the faculty member* (if you live nearby or can make a visit). If you cannot meet, then ask if you could arrange a meeting to speak with them by phone or Skype (preferably Skype). Work as much within their schedule as possible *and try to meet in person if at all possible*; it does make a difference. You get a better sense of each other, you're more likely to meet other faculty and even get a tour of the department while you're there, and they are far more likely to remember you when you do apply.

It is perfectly appropriate, and a good idea, to ask if you can send them your resume or CV if you have one. (A CV is a Curriculum Vita, which lists your undergrad degree(s), publications, any presentations you've given in pub-lic, employment and references.) You can also offer to send anything you've published that may be relevant, (as long as it isn't just a class paper; even undergraduate theses should not be sent unless a faculty member requests it, which they may if it's particularly interesting to them, but it probably won't be). But if you have published an article, by all means, mention it. If they'd like to read it, they'll let you know.

Then, after you've set up a date to meet or speak by phone, here's what you do. Reply by thanking them to agree to meet with you (or politely thank them for their time if they cannot or will not; if it's cannot, but they seem genuinely interested but just not available, let them know you'll try again in the near future at a more convenient time). Confirm in your email that you will call or meet with them at such and such a time. You want to mention the agreed upon date and time in case there was any confusion.

Keep in mind time zone changes—don't refer to your time zone; if you live on the East Coast and they live on the West, tell them you will call them at noon, their time. That means you will call them at 9:00 a.m. your time, but don't point this fact out, unless it's to explain why you can't call them at their suggested 8:00 a.m. time, because it will be 5:00 a.m. your time. Just be clear on what time in your time zone you need to call, and be clear with them on what time in their time zone to expect hearing from you.

Then unless the meeting is within a few days, send a reminder the day before. Then arrive or call them on time, as scheduled. Don't call five minutes later, and don't call five minutes before. Be as prompt as you can be. And be prepared for them to ask if they can call you back or have you wait in the hall—they might have a student in their office, they might be talking with a colleague and need to wrap it up, or they might be in the middle of writing something. But if they don't call you back when they said they would, then call them back.

How they respond to you in this early stage will give you a taste, but not necessarily any certainty, of how they will respond to you once you are a graduate student. If they show no interest or enthusiasm in your application, if they are just way too busy and show no respect for your time, then no matter how much you might think they're the best professor for you, that is probably how they will treat you once you get there. But they may also just be overwhelmed and/or caught at a bad time, so give them the benefit of the doubt unless the cool reception persists.

When you meet them or talk with them, remind them of your background. If you wrote in the email that you were a graduate of Harvard, they will probably remember (unless you are applying to Harvard yet again, in which case, you're just a local). But if you wrote that you went to Coyote College and worked in a computer software company for a couple of years, and spent a year in Italy, they very well may have forgotten everything other than you want to go to grad school. *Don't assume they remember anything about you—for the whole first year.* Well, okay, it may not be that bad, but sometimes it is; just remind them of your background very, very briefly, or pepper your conversation so very lightly with, "after I graduated from Coyote, I blah blah."

Be prepared for the conversation. You'd be amazed at how few students actually take the time to know anything about the people they want to help them. As I've said before, know what they have written and what they teach and what they are doing. (If there was something very recent or really relevant that they did and you can't find it, it is perfectly fine to ask them to send you a copy and most times they will, in which case be sure that you read it.)

If you don't already know, ask them what they will be researching/teaching in the next year. If you already know, ask them about it. Ask them if they are working with any graduate students, or if they are accepting any. Let the conversation flow naturally and see where the faculty member takes it, but also show that you have come prepared with questions.

Demonstrate your enthusiasm for graduate school, education, and the topic that interests you. But do not come across as too arrogant, smarter than they are (even if you are), too obsequious and brown-nosing, or too dead set on a specific topic or theoretical perspective that there's no sense in talking you into considering anything else.

Let them know if you need funding. Ask them about opportunities for graduate assistantships. There are usually two types of graduate assistantships: teaching assistants, and research assistants. There are sometimes also administrative assistant positions available that can be anything from secretarial work to real administrative opportunities, but they are usually appointed through research assistant positions, and usually found in interdisciplinary institutions and centers, not departments. (More about these in the section on funding your graduate education.)

If you have any special circumstances, such as you are a single mom or support your parents or just got out of prison, let them know. Remember, almost every grad student they encounter is a hardship case, so you don't want to come across as whining about being broke like everyone else, but if you really can't go to grad school unless it's funded, it helps that they know this so that if they want you in the department, they can also pitch you as a deserving candidate for any departmental scholarships or assistantship positions.

If they are doing something really exciting and you really want to work with them, consider offering to work as their research assistant over the summer preceding admissions. Say you are happy to work without pay for the opportunity and experience, because once school starts you may not have time to do so unless you are funded with an assistantship. Many graduate students get their start by volunteering for a professor, and then when there are funds available, their professor fights to get them paid. *If you aren't willing to work without pay, however, you may want to rethink graduate school.* It's a training stage and you are not only expected to seek out opportunities to gain experience and knowledge—such as volunteering—but you will ultimately advance faster and gain more almost every time you do. (If you are willing to volunteer, but unable due to other obligations, perhaps you can explain that you are working full time or have small children but would be happy to help on a particular paper or specific project, something limited but which demonstrates your commitment.)

Ask if the faculty member has any project funds to hire a graduate assistant. Notice I didn't say any funds to help you out. The focus here is on their needs, not yours. You want to express your interest in whether or not the faculty member needs an assistant, not on whether or not the faculty member can meet your needs. If they don't, then shift from their needs, to the needs of others. Don't be shy about asking if they can recommend any other faculty you might talk to who may need assistants. By coming across as eager to hear their recommendations, rather than asking who you should hit up next, and being eager to work and help out and learn, rather than desperate for money, you will impress the faculty—even though they understand you need the money.

If you have glaring weaknesses, such as a low GPA or you've been out of school awhile, address it. Don't bring attention to minor weaknesses unnecessarily, but if your GPA is below the minimum GPA or just barely hits it, or one or more of your admission test scores are really dismal, you probably should address it. Explain why you had that low GPA, but don't say you were stoned for four years. You can admit to being immature, disorganized, had family obligations, worked full time, were ill or just didn't take your studies seriously enough. But saying you have ADHD, don't consider a GPA a real measure of your achievements, were discriminated against or went to a really bad school, won't impress them, even if those things are true and did impact your grades.

I realize ADHD is considered a disability, but faculty usually find it is a diagnosis that pretty much any student can get and once you graduate, you're expected to focus and meet deadlines, regardless of your limitations. Revealing an ADHD diagnosis is likely to be interpreted as saying you won't be able to do either. Keep it to yourself, at least until you get through the door. Don't say you were hung-over when you took your admission exams. Say something like you recognize you didn't do as well on the quantitative section, and that your realize your strengths are more qualitative. Don't say you went to a bad school, even if you did—that will mean you aren't well educated. And don't say you were discriminated against; they're not likely to buy it, even if true (and in academia, it's often true). Let them draw those conclusions. Take responsibility for that low grade point or that low admissions test score, no matter what the reasons. But that doesn't mean you can't offer an explanation.

There is a whole range of attitudes to GPA's and admissions test scores and as a rule, the more quantitative and scientific the department, the more important the scores. But if you have a weakness in your scores or GPA it always helps for someone to understand the reason why. I once sat in on a meeting where a student with a near perfect GRE score was not going to be admitted to the program because in his last year of undergrad he had flunked every course he took one semester (faculty are more forgiving of students who mess up early on but get their act together in their last two years). Fortunately, he'd explained to one of the faculty members his reason: his sister was murdered that semester and he was too traumatized to finish. Unfortunately, it was a rigid department consisting mostly of old fools and simple minds, so even with a few of us supporting him, the majority still rejected him. The moral? Faculty can't fight for you and explain away your weaknesses if you haven't explained them yourself. And if you have a legitimate reason but still don't get in, you might want to thank your lucky stars you didn't end up with such foolish people influencing your career.

When you meet with faculty, keep the conversation a reasonable length (about twenty minutes is reasonable; hopefully it will go longer and it may be only ten minutes). Be sensitive to any cues the faculty member is giving that they need to get going, and help them wrap it up. If you are meeting in person, be sure to take note of any insight you gain about their personal interests—photos, décor, knick knacks—whatever gives you either conversational openers, establishes rapport, or gives you insight into your compatibility, will help.

Thank them before you leave; ask if you can follow up if you have any additional questions, and then, later in the evening or the following day, drop them a thank you email or a handwritten card.

Then contact them a couple of weeks later (not too soon) by sending them an interesting news article, a question (if it pertains to something you learn about the department or university, then it's fine to follow up sooner), or commenting on something you read about. Reiterate your interest in working with them, but don't overdo it. The key is to not be a pest, but to be sure they don't forget you. It is helpful here to remind them, such as, "We spoke a few weeks ago about my interest in applying for the graduate program, and I mentioned my interest in Nonsensical Mish Mash. I just came across this article by Dr. Delirious on blah blah and thought I'd share it with you in case it's of interest to you and you haven't already seen it. Looking forward to talking again, sincerely, Eager Student."

It's perfectly fine to ask them for two or three recommended readings; it is not fine to expect them to do your research for you or tell you who the main theorists are in a topic you've already said you are very interested in. If you are so interested, you should already know who they are. Just show that you will read anything they might send you, and if they send you anything, be sure you do read it.

And then *drop them a line or a visit once more before you send in the application*, unless you'd come across like a stalker if you did so. The goal is that they remember you favorably and are happy to have you join them.

Chapter 7

● ● ●

GET YOUR REFERENCES IN ORDER

Alright, now you're almost ready to apply. But you are going to need three or more letters of reference *(send whatever number the application requests, no more, no less)*. The key here is to remember that a strong letter from a complete unknown is better than a mediocre letter from Stephen Hawking. Well, maybe a mediocre letter from Stephen Hawking is better than an outstanding one from your English teacher, but the general rule is, go for the strongest letters, not the strongest names.

If you are currently in an undergraduate program or have recently graduated, and aren't quite ready to apply to grad school, do keep in touch with your professors. Drop them greetings during the holidays or just drop by their office (during office hours) or drop them a line, updating them as to what you've been up to professionally. Read what they are publishing and comment favorably on their work. Maintain the relationship, but don't be a pest. Let them know you will eventually be applying for graduate school, and ask if they have any graduate programs they'd recommend. And always thank them for their time (I know I'm repeating myself, but it's startling how often people fail to thank others for their time and assistance.)

If you've been out for some time or just don't have faculty contacts, consider taking a seminar or two to get to know some faculty. But don't despair if you aren't able to do that. In addition to current or former professors, employers, supervisors of anything you worked on or volunteered with, and well-healed family connections are always good choices for letters of references.

When you contact the people who you will be asking for reference letters, tell them you are applying for graduate school and ask if they would be comfortable writing a letter of recommendation for you. *Tell them exactly when it is due*, and be sure it is not the following day. If you ask too far in advance, they will probably put it off, so you'll have to remind them again as the clock draws near. If you ask them on too short notice, they won't be happy. Try to aim for one month advance notice if you can.

Tell them what you've been up to since you last spoke, why you want to go to graduate school (and why a particular discipline and school), and what your career aspirations are. *Don't assume they remember much about you or your education, no matter how well they knew you or how many classes you took.* Remind them of exactly what classes you took, what papers you wrote, what grades you received, or what projects you worked on. If you still have any papers or letters or anything that could revitalize their memories, even if it was just the previous month, send a copy. Even if they know you well, the more specific examples you can remind them of, the more specific they can be in their letters. If your professor gushed about how much he or she loved a paper you did, say something like, "You really liked my paper on blah blah." Be tactful, provide any useful details, but don't make it sound like you are telling them what to write.

But it is fine to frame your request for a reference letter in such a way that helps nudge them in the direction you want them to go. Don't tell them what to write, but wherever you can make your case for admission based on the experience the professor has had with you, the better. For example, supposing you had done a complex research project for them; you could say something like, "I'm hoping to demonstrate that I'm experienced with research and since I learned so much from the project I did for you on the history of the future, I thought you'd have the best sense of my skills in that area."

But keep in mind, professors can be treacherous. Even the worst don't want to tell you they think you're a dim bulb or a nut case who doesn't belong in college. Some will tell you that, and they may or may not be wrong. But *far too many will agree to write you a letter, and then write a mediocre or damning letter.* I have known professors who assured their students they would be happy to write them letters, only to turn around and advise potential employers not to hire them. I have even had to write letters myself for students who were very likable, but only average students. In those cases, it's hard to say no; you don't want to hurt their feelings. So while talking with the student I've expressed any reservations I've had with their work, listened to their responses, and then when writing the letter done my best to be tactful, address the student's shortcomings, but focus the letter on their strengths and potential.

So if you are not a stellar student, a good way to avoid such a hazard is to come right out and *ask the person if they have any concerns that would prevent them from writing a strong letter.* If you know for a fact that they do, address it up front. Explain to them that you realize you were not the best student in the past, but you have matured and gained experience. Watch their body language to see how uncomfortable they are with the conversation. If they are negative, discouraging, and/or turn away from you or shake their head while assuring you that they'd write you a good letter, beware. But usually if you come right out and ask about their concerns, they'll be honest with you. *Don't argue with them; listen to them.* Even if they are wrong, they are telling you why they would hesitate to write you a strong letter and you can do one of two things: address their concerns in a responsible manner that shows you understand them and are a new and improved version of your former self, or get another person to write the letter.

Sometimes a professor, or other referee, will ask that that you write the letter of reference and they will sign it. In fact, that request is a lot more common than you might think. Personally, I am no fan of that approach. It tells the student that they aren't worth the faculty member's time, demands of the student that they extol their own virtues which a narcissist will overdo and someone with low self-esteem will poorly do, and it means that the letter probably won't sound at all like a professional reference. It will probably read like a letter an undergrad wrote.

If that happens, be honest. Tell them you'd be uncomfortable doing that and if they still insist, either find someone else to write the letter or have someone else ghostwrite the letter for you to submit to the professor (choose someone in a professional capacity who knows you well enough to write a strong letter, but isn't another one of your referees).

For all your referees, *don't make them look stuff up.* Provide them any form they need to fill out and sign, but do not include a stamped envelope. They will either scan the form and letter and email it directly, or send it in a university or corporate envelope (but if you are asking someone who is not affiliated with a university or business, and just sending it from home, then it is appropriate to include a stamped addressed envelope).

About two weeks before the letter is due, send them a gentle reminder. But before you do, check in with the university you are applying to (there is usually a place online that you can log into, or you can just call the graduate school or department) to be sure all your letters have arrived. *Then when the letter has arrived, send a thank you note.*

If you're reaching the deadline and the letter hasn't been received and the professor is missing in action or blowing you off (which is often the case, especially because so many application deadlines are during the winter break when faculty are gone), then hustle up a backup letter from wherever you can find it. Call them. Drop in at their office if it's nearby. Contact the department chair or administrative assistant where the missing professor works to see if they are in town and checking their emails. Then if you still can't find them, get your backup letter, even if it's not what you were hoping for. The important thing is to get a completed application in by the deadline.

But suppose you don't have any former professors who would remember you, or if they did, it wouldn't be good. Or your former professor who you worked so closely with has died. If it is the latter, be sure to mention it in your letter of application. I was once on a search committee for a job candidate and one of the things that really stood out was that although her letters of recommendation were very good, she didn't have one from her main advisor. That was a very big red flag and nearly cost her the interview because if the person who worked with her most closely didn't vouch for her, there may have been good reason. Fortunately, her application was so strong otherwise that someone finally just sent her an email asking about it. It turned out that her advisor had died, but she hadn't told us that. Knowing that detail made all the difference in the world, and she was invited for a campus interview. So if you have a dead advisor, be sure to mention it.

That said, most likely you had no advisor at all or if you did, there's always the chance that they have forgotten you or they would only send a half-hearted letter or none at all or they have good cause not to like you. Remember, a strong letter from nobody beats a weak letter from somebody, so move on to someone else. Is there an employer or someone you worked or volunteered with who can write you a letter? A friend who is successfully employed? A friend who will fake it? I once had a friend who wanted to go to graduate school but had been out of school and unemployed for so long that he couldn't come up with anyone impressive to write his letters. So I wrote a brilliant letter extolling his virtues, and mentioning all the excellent research and writing he had done for me, put it on some fancy letterhead and signed my name followed by "Ph.D." Now that would have been perfectly acceptable, except for the fact that at that point in time, not only did I not have a Ph.D., but it had never even occurred to me that one day I would have one, and he had never done any work with or for me. It was a complete snow job but he got admitted to grad school.

But don't do anything like that unless it's the very last option. And if you do, and you do get in, never let on that you submitted a phony letter—especially to your grad school colleagues and preferably not even to your spouse (things get ugly if you get divorced). You don't want anyone ever having a reason to toss you out the door if they decide that they don't like you, so keep it to yourself, at least until you're long gone. (And if you do get into grad school, or anywhere, based on a phony reference, never run for public office. The truth will hit you in the face one day. Do your best to keep it honest.)

If you are still stuck and don't have anyone to write you any letters, how much more time do you have before they're due? If you've started the application process early on, then you may still have time to do some volunteering for someone and they may write a letter. If that is the case, opt for the bigger name and the mediocre (or hopefully, not so mediocre) letter. No one can write you an outstanding letter if they don't really know you, but if you volunteer for a few months to do some research or writing or whatever for someone with a well-known reputation and you do an excellent job, they may be quite happy to write a letter about what excellent work you did and how delightful you were to work with even if they've only known you a few months.

Finally, if you are a complete unknown with no friends or virtues, get a fake address and letterhead and write your own letters. Make sure the writing style and fonts are different in each one and there are no grammatical errors or misspellings. You will probably get caught, but if things are that bad, what have you got to lose? You won't go to jail for it, you just won't go to grad school, at least not yet. But never give up, another year and you'll be amazed what new friends and accomplishments you may be enjoying, so persevere, my friend, persevere!

Chapter 8

● ● ●

WRITE (OR BUY) THE ESSAY

Now it's time to write the make-it or break-it application essay. Although some faculty don't even bother to read the essays, focusing exclusively on the test scores, GPA, undergraduate institution and letters of reference, most faculty pay close attention to the personal essay. There is no underestimating its importance; a badly written one can tank a brilliant student's admission, and a well-written one might just get a drug-addled moron into the Ivy Leagues. So don't wait until the last minute to write it, unless you are your most brilliant under pressure.

There are three main types of essays that end up tossed out immediately (unless the university is desperate for grad students or the applicant is well connected to a potential donor or sleeping with the faculty). These three are:

The enthusiastic student who is fascinated by everything. You know what I mean, the student who is so eager to get in that they enthuse about how anything the faculty teach will fascinate them and they are open to studying anything the faculty want them to study because they find absolutely everything so fascinating. That may well be true, and the genuinely intelligent and intellectually curious student does find almost everything intriguing. But the Ivory Towers are not the place for the genuinely intelligent or the intellectually curious, who tend to get in and get out as quickly as possible. Universities are a far better depository for the shrewd and the clever and those with above-average intelligence but no real originality or depth (not that we're talking about you. We're talking about those other people. The ones who'll be your grad school colleagues and professors). If someone does have the former qualities of intellect and depth, they are likely socially inept and hence not bothering with graduate admissions. So show some focus.

The other type of essay that gets tossed out is just the opposite. And that is: *The student who is so focused that they already know exactly what they will do during their graduate studies, have already made up their minds about everything the faculty have to teach them and they just want to get in and be left alone to write that brilliant thesis on Nonsensical Mumbo Jumbo.* This is the student who may well have done their homework, and in many cases may know more about the topic than the faculty (but probably doesn't know a damn thing). This is also a student who will be a drag to teach because they are not interested in learning; they're more interested in showing off what they think they've already learned. If you present yourself as already smart enough to start the thesis, and so narrowly focused on what you are going to study that there is no room for intellectual growth or new directions, unless you already have a cozy relationship with a faculty member who wants you working with them, you are unlikely to get in. You want to demonstrate focus, but flexibility and a desire to learn what the faculty have to offer.

And what the faculty have to offer gets us to the third type of essay that gets tossed out, and that is from: *The student who has no idea what the department has to offer, and is clearly sending out a generic letter to every university in the nation with no clue that the department does not have a single course or faculty member who specializes or gives a damn about the terribly dated or irrelevant or just off the wall topic the student has declared they want to study.* Demonstrate that you know something about the department, its faculty, its reputation and its graduate programs. Faculty are well aware that you are applying to other departments, but they want to believe that theirs is your first choice, or at least a department you'd be thrilled and honored to join. If it's clear you didn't take the time to even look at their website, what are the chances that you'll take the time to do good work?

Naturally, any essay that is poorly written and chock full of misspellings and grammatical errors and comes across as goofy will be tossed. Be sure it demonstrates that you are college educated and ready for graduate studies. Don't ask a bunch of rhetorical questions; be sure all your sentences end with periods, not question marks (and certainly not exclamation points, which make you sound like a gushing teenager). Don't cuss. Don't bad-mouth your former university. Humor rarely works in personal essays, mostly because it's usually badly done. Unless you're a gifted and subtle humorist, leave the wise-cracks out. (Just look at me, I'm funny and they tossed my ass out of the Ivory Towers, no doubt because I wasn't sufficiently droll.)

Read the instructions for the essay, and clearly answer any questions that it poses. If it tells you to explain why you want to go to graduate school, don't say something as meaningless as you want to keep on learning. That's too vague. Show that you have given some thought to what you want to do with your life and what you want to learn and what you want to be when you grow up. Be general enough to show you don't yet have all the answers, but focused enough to have an idea what direction you want to go in.

Tell them why you want to go to graduate school and what your career objectives are. If you are applying for a Master's degree but plan to go on for a Ph.D., say so. Of if you plan to get in and get out, it's fine to say you would like to complete your M.S. degree and go into private practice counseling repentant attorneys if that's your objective. The point is, show that you have goals, direction, and a desire to learn. And show that to reach those goals, you need a graduate education. You do not need to be, nor should you be, too focused. But to the extent you can show that your intellectual interests are consistent with the faculty's, the better your chances of admission.

It's here that your conversations with the faculty may have revealed some potential directions—for example, if a professor indicated the department was building up its program in Nonsensical Mumbo Jumbo and it fits with your interests, say that's what you want to do. If it turns out not to be something that you want to stick with, you can always change directions once you get there. The point is to get in.

Likewise, if a professor told you they'd be thrilled to work with you, or even they just reluctantly agreed to it, mention your interest in working with them. For example, in your essay clearly state that you would like to study Metaphysical Chemistry under the mentorship of Professor Esoterica. Professor Esoterica will be sure to discuss his or her interest in working with you in the faculty meeting, but if you don't mention it, he or she might feel snubbed, or they may not remember you and their interest in working with you may not even come up.

Alright, by this point some of you will be saying, "You said not to say we wanted to study under so and so because we need to get to know them for a semester, and now you say we should say so in the personal statement; which is it?" You got me. Both answers are true. That is because it's a treacherous game, and you need to know how to play it. You very well may want to study with a particular professor and they also want to work with you and that is perfectly fine and you should say so in your letter. But once you get into the program, be sure you continue to forge relationships with other faculty in case your favorite professor turns out to be Mommy Dearest, which very often is the case.

On the other hand, if you really aren't sure who you want to study with and no one has taken you under their wing, or at least, no one whose wings you want as shelter, then you simply say you are interested in studying abstract realism under the guidance of Professors Esoterica and Pseudoscientifica. List the two or three faculty whose interests overlap with yours, rather than just one professor, and you are fine. Try something like, "I am particularly excited about the possibility of studying in your department given the faculty strengths in my area of interest. For example, Professor Pseudoscientifica's work in astroastrology and Professor Esoterica's research in All Things Best Forgotten, are directly related to my interest in New Age Forensic studies."

The essay is also where your prior perusal of the university website comes in. Weave in some buzzwords from the Strategic Plan and Mission Statement, but don't be too obvious. Don't say you are interested in advancing knowledge, diversifying the student body or globalizing your vision. But if they are going in the direction of "building bridges to the community," see what the economic base, the environmental problems, or the demographics of the local community actually are. If you are going to study something related to the environment and you can show that you are interested in local water quality issues, and you happen to have read in the local paper that water quality is a big concern, then you're showing you are relevant and have done your homework.

Similarly, if the economic base of the community is based in the health fields, the military, or technology, for example, and your potential research is related to such issues, say that you are interested in working in those areas or that among your interests would be exploring opportunities to conduct research related to the nearby think tank/transnational corporation/military industrial complex or whatever it is the university website says it is "partnering" with.

Don't present yourself as a potential threat to any of these institutions or organizations, such as saying you want to do some muckraking and investigate what they are up to, but just show some respect for local community issues and interest in exploring research possibilities. It does not mean that's what you have to do once you get there; you can always change your mind and your research focus. But it does show you are aware of what is going on, you are creative in recognizing opportunities and could potentially be engaged in research that could benefit the university or at the very least you just might find some local funding once you do get started on your research. Also, faculty throughout the university will be engaged in research projects related to whatever organization or institution the university is involved in, and they may have research funds to help you. So just consider ways you might be able to get involved in such projects, if they are relevant to you.

If you saw that they are planning to increase funding to a certain area, and you have an interest in doing research in that direction, emphasize that interest. If you want to work internationally and you saw that they are moving toward "globalizing" the university (and they all are), then say you are interested in international work and mention any foreign languages you speak and any foreign travel or living you have done (you should mention these things, regardless, unless it was just a quick weekend in the Caribbean and gave you no real international exposure).

Discuss your previous education, work experience, volunteer work and, again, travel. These things are very important, and often overlooked. Even the Ivy

Leagues are increasingly accepting graduate students who have demonstrated some life skills and concern for social issues, over the students who have the top scores and GPA but are only interested in making money. *Emphasize anything you have done related to citizenship, social justice, and community.* Don't try to be pretentious or write in a manner that is unfamiliar to you, but *write professionally and demonstrate confidence, goals, experience and a desire to learn.*

Make sure you mention any research projects you worked on, and any professional presentations you gave. Research experience is particularly important in the STEM fields, but in any program, if you conducted independent research and/or helped a professor or anyone else with a research project, discuss it. What was the project? What was your role? What were the findings? Was anything published as a result of the project? Even if your name wasn't on it, if you helped a professor with research related to something they published, make sure you discuss it. And do your best to get that professor to write one of your letters of recommendation, and note in their letter your role (in the section on reference letters, I discuss how to approach these professors). And if you gave any public talks, or presentations, such as at a professional conference, be sure to include it.

Another important part of the essay will be your biography. Some universities will just want one single essay that includes some discussion of your background, while others will require a separate essay. Either way, this is where you have an opportunity to present any hardships or obstacles you have overcome to get to where you are today. *If you are the first in your family to go to college, say so,* and explain what inspired you to do so. Are you a single parent? Raised by a single parent? Have you had a family member with a disability that sensitized you to the challenges others face in life? *Show how the obstacles in your life have taught and inspired you and challenged you to be creative in troubled times.*

Include your achievements, which are not just honors and awards and grades and degrees—all good and to be mentioned for sure—but also tell them about anything you are proud about regarding your character, what you have learned, or skills you have mastered. Don't underestimate the value of any hobbies. Many students are admitted based on a faculty member being fascinated about their personal interests. I wouldn't advise discussing hobbies that might come across as less than intellectual, such as reading tarot cards or watching TV, but if you have musical abilities, engage in interactive gaming, design anything, climb rocks, build furniture, or sail, you might want to say so. But make sure you present your hobby in the best light—don't come across as someone who is addicted to gaming, for example. But if you can discuss gaming in a manner which displays your intellect, creativity and vision, then you're more likely to impress them. Don't talk about your love of knitting dog sweaters, but if you can discuss how knitting has taught you patience and attention to detail, then you're giving them a vision of you as a future student—not as a dog knitter.

If you have been influenced by someone—in your life, work or intellectually—tell them about it if you think it is relevant to your education.

Tell your story. It's really that simple (and that difficult). Stories have beginnings, middles and ends. They have protagonists—the main character—and that's you. The protagonist is in search of something—not just a degree, but what that degree will bring you—but in seeking that goal, the protagonist encounters obstacles along the way. Tell that story, the story of you seeking wisdom, purpose, identity, and what steps you have taken to attain those goals and what unexpected obstacles have gotten in the way and how you've overcome them.

As with any story, show, don't tell. Never tell them you're a perfect fit for their department; that's for them to determine. Show you are a good fit by using their language, by being the person they are looking for, by demonstrating that you can write, that you have impressive achievements, that you are a critical thinker, that you are humble yet confident, that you will be a joy to have around. Never say those things, but show it in the story you tell them about yourself. Let them like you. And then let them see you there, in their minds, working with them and being there physically and socially.

If there are any interdisciplinary centers or research institutes at the university that you want to work with, say so. If you have spoken to the directors in these units, say so. It probably won't make any real difference, but it will contribute to the overall image you are projecting of having done your homework and having a direction and being a part of the university.

And don't tell them they're a great university. They know that, even if they're a crappy university. You can conclude with some language about it being an honor if you are accepted to their university or some such thing, but don't heap on the praise. Be respectful, show that you are impressed by the university, its faculty, and the resources the university and department have to offer, but don't suck up, don't state the obvious, and don't tell them anything they already know. Stand out by telling them about you and do it in such a way that they will conclude you belong there and they want to have you around.

In order to stand out, avoid sounding like all the other essays they will read. There has been so much written about starting the personal essay with a question, that the minute you do that you sound like all the others. "What does it take to become a gifted teacher?" is not a good opening line if you are applying for a graduate degree in education. It's too simplistic and too common.

Don't open with a question because either it's rhetorical and will make you sound less mature and professional, or you're going to answer it, which means you've wasted all those words that could have been put to better use. Opening with a question did at one time set you apart; now it's so overdone it comes across as a gimmick. Avoid it unless you're a really clever writer.

Don't open with "Ever since I was a child" or variations of the "Ever since I was" meme, such as "From an early age" or "For as long as I can recall."

Never start with a word or two followed by a comma; dive right into the sentence. Commas chop up sentences, so use them sparingly.

Don't start with "Currently I am . . ." as in, "Currently I am finishing up my degree in Mumbo-Jumbo," which is boring and more common than commas. (Clearly you want to say that at some point in the essay, but it's not a good opener.)

Never start by telling them what they already know about the profession, as in "Philosophy requires a deep understanding of the classics," "Law is the cornerstone to our democracy," or "Hocus Pocus is a demanding career requiring an in-depth mastery of magic and razzle dazzle." You are wasting your limited words and not impressing them every time you tell them something obvious.

Beginning with or even including phrases such as "I am fascinated by," "it is my dream to," or "I am passionate about" are all trite, exaggerated and overused. Avoid them. Show, don't tell. Show them your fascination or dream or passion by writing about it and how you came to gain that fascination, dream or passion. *Show, don't tell.*

Feel free to include a mention or anecdote from your childhood, but *don't overly focus on your childhood or high school years.* Let them see you as a maturing, professional adult.

To do so, don't come across like a gushing teenager. Words like awesome, unbelievable, amazing and passion, are so overused that you'll immediately lose your luster once you use them.

The worst opening line is, "I will never forget . . ." Don't say you will never forget something or that you will always remember something, as in "I will never forget the day I first realized I wanted to be an astronaut," or "I will always remember my first day of Kindergarten." Similarly, "I've wanted to be an astronaut ever since I was a child," is a lukewarm opening. Try something more distinctive, like "I didn't start out wanting to fly into outer space. If anything, watching the night sky as a child wasn't nearly as interesting as watching, yet again, the latest remake of *Star Wars* and imagining myself engaged in preposterous intergalactic battles with super-powered villains. But while taking an introductory class in physics in my freshman year in college, my understanding of the universe changed profoundly." That's an introduction that instantly sets you apart from all the others who always wanted to be astronauts since they were children and were inspired by Hollywood movies that are so far afield from real life that they're bound to be disappointed and bored by the real thing.

Anytime your inspiration comes from Hollywood, you're marking yourself as ordinary and unimaginative (unless, of course, you're applying to film school in which case, dive right in, but be specific about your influences and goals). If Hollywood really did inspire you to move into a particular career, what else has shaped your understanding of the field? In what ways have you moved beyond the fictional world of movies and television to gain a more realistic perception of what that career will require and entail?

Another common theme is how special grandma or grandpa were and what an inspiration they were to you. Don't write about your grandparents, unless you've got a killer anecdote to tell (you could say you were raised by your grandparents if that was the case, but for the most part, grandparents are in every other essay, so keep yours out).

Generally it's a bad idea to start with a quote, unless it's a really good, really salient one—and not one that's been used so many times it's meaningless. The very worst quotes are on the order of "If life gives you lemons," "Keep calm and carry on," "Be the change you wish to see in the world," "Shoot for the moon, even if you miss you'll land among the stars." Heard it before? Then so have they.

Don't say you want to make a difference, think outside the box, or give back to your community/society/family for all you've received. More clichés. *Any phrase you've heard before is a cliché and your reader's read it before. Use original language.*

But most important of all is not to worry about the opening line or lines. Just start writing; you can write the opening later, but if you sit there staring at a blank page trying to come up with something that will grab the faculty's attention and wow them, then you're likely to keep staring. Just start writing. Pretend you're writing an email to someone who has asked you, "Why do you want to go to graduate school, and why at that place?"

Finally, if you can't write so much as a Twitter post, hire someone else to write your entrance essay (but you're on your own once you get in; you may be able to hire people to do most if not all of your work through graduate school, but faculty will probably catch on. Even if they don't, unless you're a mad scientist and only communicate in numbers, if you depend on others to write your work when you are in graduate school, you might not belong there).

Others may disagree with me, but in my view, having someone ghost-write your admissions essay is not the same as having them write your papers. *You absolutely should write your own essay,* but I've seen too many excellent candidates get rejected because they didn't know how to market themselves and write a sales pitch. So if you are lousy at that sort of thing, or English is your second language, don't despair. You're not alone and it's something you can learn, or buy. Look on line; there are plenty of places that do that sort of thing, and you can always find someone on Craigslist. Ask how many grad school application essays they write each year and what percentage get into the school of their choice. They may not answer truthfully, but listen closely to *how* they answer you. Ask if they will revise it after you read the first draft, and if so, if that is an extra cost. You want someone who will keep revising it until it's an essay you're comfortable with submitting.

What kinds of questions do they ask you? Do they take the time to learn your story and your interests? Or do they only want to know your GPA and test scores, spend little time talking with you, and then tell you they'll have your letter done in a few days? If that's the case, it's probably a stock letter. You want someone who will spend time with you, who will spend time looking at the university website or carefully review the information you give them about the department's mission, the faculty specializations, and the institutions and research centers that will be relevant to you. But be prepared to pay several hundred dollars for an experienced essay writer. The cheaper they are, the more likely they're inexperienced, though as with any service, even the costly ones can be bad, and an inexpensive one could prove to be a gem. Check out a few different ones and go with the one that spends the most time talking with you and wants to know about where you are applying, why you are applying, and who you are.

Once you've finished your essay, review the requirements again to be sure you've touched all the bases. Then if you know anyone who is or has been a professor or admissions counselor at a university or college, and can review your entrance letter, have them read it. Based on the feedback you get from other professionals, and from a review of the guidelines they require, revise your essay. *An essay that is not revised is a mediocre essay.* All good writers revise what they write and if you're too wedded to your words or overconfident in what you've said, chances are you haven't done as good a job as you can and worse, will struggle once you're in grad school. The smarter you are, the more open you'll be to revising your work.

As you review your essay, ask yourself the following questions.

- Have you addressed every question or topic they've listed?
- Are your sentences too long? *The average sentence length a person can read before it becomes confusing is 16 words.* Sentences longer than that are best broken into two or more sentences.
- Do you have paragraph breaks? Keep your essay readable by using paragraph breaks. *If you are submitting your essay electronically, use even more paragraph breaks* because depending on how it is delivered, the screen they read from may be smaller. If that is the case, short paragraphs help make the text more readable.
- Are you repetitive? Say it once, then move on.
- Are you using clichés? As I've said before, if it's an expression you've heard before, don't use it. Be original.
- Are you overly effusive? Show you know the department and university by discussing specific faculty, course offerings and programs. Don't gush. They don't want you telling them the obvious, which is that if you got into their program it would be great! But it does help to say you'd be honored to be admitted, and to demonstrate your knowledge of what it is about them that makes them such a good fit for you.
- Do you have incomplete sentences? Do you swear? Do you use quotation marks? Most times quotation marks look ridiculous. *Unless it's dialogue or the title to an article, take out the quotation marks.* Did you try making your points through rhetorical questions? I hope not. Once again, and I repeat myself because rhetorical questions are so common and so ill advised, if you pose a question, suggest an answer (and then re-read the sentence to see if you can drop the question altogether). Don't just toss off something to sound cute, like "What better way to learn than through failure?" or "Who needs perfect grades anyway?" Rhetorical questions mark you as naïve. Delete them.
- Take out all the exclamation points! Unless you are scolding someone or writing dialogue and it's a teenager speaking, take them out! I mean it!

- Have you clearly articulated what you want to study, why you want to study it, and what you've done to prepare for it?
- Have you been specific about your strengths, achievements and qualities, or have you been vague? Give specific examples.
- Does your essay flow logically? Can you summarize each paragraph in a line and from that list of lines, see a progression? If not, reread it closely to see if and how you can improve it.
- Are you concise? Do you keep within the word limit and use those words effectively? Don't ramble or chatter. Get to the point.
- Do you refer to the university you are sending it off to, but not to any other university? It's quite common for people to write a single essay and send it to multiple universities, not closely reviewing it to be sure there are no references to the wrong university. *Be sure any references to a university, department or program you are applying to refer only to the one you are submitting it to.*
- Never ever send it off until you have proofread it for misspellings, typos, grammatical errors and any other mistakes. Then let it sit for twenty-four hours and proof it again. And make sure every sentence contains a verb. Incomplete sentences are dreadful. Use verbs (and limit the adjectives and adverbs).

Most importantly, be sure it gets there on time. Contact the department a couple of days before the deadline to be sure they have all of your application materials.

Chapter 9

● ● ●

TAKE (OR DON'T TAKE) THE ENTRANCE EXAMS

Now this is a chapter that should have come much earlier, because you need to take these exams at an early stage. But if I'd put this chapter up front, you'd have tossed the book out and cursed me for drowning you in details. But these are important details, so think of them like eating your veggies. They're good for you. Better yet, think of them like mixed vegetables, and only pick out the ones you want. In other words, skim past the discussions about exams that don't relate to what you're going into, but do read up on what does apply. You will probably need to take an entrance exam to get in, and you will want to score as high as possible.

High scores can make a huge difference. When Julie Posselt, a professor of higher education at the University of Michigan sat in on the admission committees of ten doctoral programs at three different universities to find out just what got students admitted—or rejected—she discovered that a high GRE score could compensate for an awful lot. In her book, *Inside Graduate Admissions: Merit, Diversity and Faculty Gatekeeping* (Harvard University Press, 2016) she tells how admissions is as much about the faculty making the decisions as it is about the students they admit—and that disciplines have different ideas about how to judge merit. In the STEM (Science, Technology, Engineering and Mathematics) fields, and other programs where quantitative methods are valued, the entrance exam scores are usually highly valued.

In contrast, in the social sciences and the humanities, other factors such as the student's personal history, their community service and activities, and other personal factors may be given greater weight. And in any given department, there are some faculty for whom a high or low entrance exam score means everything, and other faculty who don't find it to be an accurate indication at all of how a student will do once admitted.

The important thing to understand is that while there are no absolutes, entrance exam scores usually count for a lot in the STEM fields. In other fields where you aren't so sure, by looking closely at what the faculty teach and publish, and what courses are required for graduation, you'll have a better sense of how much quantitative data count in the departments you're applying to. But don't assume that just because a department doesn't have much of a quantitative focus that GRE scores don't matter—for many people they do. And that means for better or worse, if you want to go to grad school you should take the GRE's (or GMAT, LSAT, or MCAT, which I discuss further on) and do as well as you possibly can—and if you can't do well, don't worry, I'll get to that part later. But whatever you do, do prepare for it. Students who study for the entrance exams do significantly better than those who do not. Moreover, international students tend to study a great deal for these exams and as a result, score quite high—and you will be competing with other applicants who have studied and scored high. So do study.

THE GRE

The Graduate Record Exams are designed to test your aptitude, intellect and ability to solve problems. (If you are applying to business school, you'll probably have to take the GMAT; for law school, the LSAT; and for medical school, the MCAT. Read this section anyway, because much of it applies to those tests, and then I'll get to the other tests.)

You take the exams on a computer, but they must be taken at an approved testing center, and you can find a testing center near you through the GRE test site (http://www.ets.org/gre/). The tests are provided year round, but since most grad schools take new students in the fall, it's best to begin preparing in early spring and take the test in late summer or early fall *the year before you hope to be admitted*. That means a year and a half in advance of admission—but if you're already running late in the application process, just take it as soon as you can but do prepare for it.

The GRE takes about four hours to complete—with short breaks, but no bathroom breaks, so go easy on the coffee (take over-the-counter caffeine pills if you need them). You can't use calculators or notes, and the smart phone stays at home, just in case Siri gets it into her head to whisper the answers to you.

And make sure that phone stays at home—I don't know about the GRE's, but I know someone who was kicked out of the SAT test after spending a couple of grueling hours on it, all because an alarm she'd forgotten to turn off had gone off.

The cost of the test, at the time of this writing (in 2016), is $160, which includes prep software, and sending the results to up to four schools. If you want to send the results to more schools, it's $23.00 for each additional one.

Now that we've got those details out of the way, just what can you expect when you take the test, aside from tedium and worry? Well there are three sections to the test: analytical, verbal and quantitative. The first part of the test is the analytical section, which is comprised of two essays. For the first essay you have 45 minutes to read and discuss it, supporting your argument with evidence gleaned from the text. The second essay takes 30 minutes and your task is to critique the argument they've presented. Now this might seem like a simple enough task, but one reading of the daily newspaper makes it pretty clear that people generally don't pay much attention to evidence in an argument, and when they critique something they tend to rely more on emotion than on the intellectual foundation of what they're critiquing.

On the other hand, I am personally of the view that anyone who actually wants to be an educated and wise person, can learn relatively easily how to read a passage, identify the evidence it presents and what evidence is missing, and critique an argument logically, once they set their emotions aside. To develop your own skills in this area, try arguing a point you disagree with.

What evidence can you find to make your point? Where do you find this evidence? How objective is the source?

Start reading in a different way. Read not to find proof of what you already believe to be true. Read to discern what the evidence is that the author presents, where that evidence comes from, and what evidence is lacking—what might someone who disagrees with the author find to be a weakness in the argument? Just as a defense attorney must think like a prosecutor to win, and a prosecutor must think like a defense attorney, so, too, must you start thinking from a different perspective in order to develop your analytical skills. The more you can argue politics without becoming angry, the closer you're getting to analyzing a position, not arguing it. Give it a shot.

But I digressed. Now, back to the GRE's. The second part you'll take is the verbal test. Like the quantitative test, which we'll get to in a minute, the verbal test will become more difficult if you're answering correctly, and less difficult if you aren't. It adjusts itself to your abilities (but don't think you can answer a few wrong just to get easier questions—they're weighted differently, so the easier the question, the fewer points you'll score).

The verbal portion of the GRE tests vocabulary, and relationships between concepts and words. It is comprised of 30 questions which you must answer in 30 minutes. If you're taking the test on paper, which is an option but I can't imagine anyone doing so, you will have two sets of 38 questions each. The more you read, the more likely you have a strong vocabulary. But if you aren't much of a reader, you may not have the vocabulary necessary to score well, so be sure you put extra time into this area (more on test prep coming up). And if English is not your native language, you may not do as well in this area, so be sure to study for this section. (You may also have to take the TOEFL exam, the Test of English as a Foreign Language, which I'll get to in the section on International Students.)

The third portion of the GRE's is the Quantitative section. This section tests you on high school level math, including algebra, geometry, and data analysis. You will have 45 minutes to answer 28 questions (or if not taking the test on a computer, you will have two sets of thirty questions with 30 minutes for each). As I noted before, you can't use calculators, so unless you're a mathematical whiz, you'll need to study!

Just how do you study? As I've said, it pays to prepare for these tests, so do spend some time on them. You can obtain free software, called Power Prep II, from the GRE test site: http://www.ets.org/gre/revised_general/prepare/ powerprep2.

For about $20, you can download software that will give you practice analytical tests based on real tests questions from this site: https://www.dxr-group.com/cgi-bin/scoreitnow/index.pl.

And there's always Kaplan and Peterson's, the industry leaders in test prep (as far as their cornering the market on this sort of thing; I have no idea whether they're useful or worth the added cost or not). As of 2016, the cost for Kaplan ranges from $699 (for self-paced) to $2,499 (private tutoring). Personally, I'd try the free software first.

Peterson's offers much more reasonably priced test prep at $19.95 for ninety days, covering 500 sample questions. Their website is a navigational nightmare, but this link should get you straight to it: https://www.petersons.com/graduate-schools/gre-practice-test.aspx.

Veritas Prep is another option, but plan to pay big money. The reviews for Veritas are strong, but costs from $1,400 for a thirty-hour course to $6,950 for private tutoring. They are planning a more affordable online, self-help option in the near future, but as of this writing it isn't yet available.

Then there's the Princeton Review. Again, I can neither endorse nor condemn them, as I know nothing about how cost-effective they are, or whether they are any better than the free software, but they offer test prep packages that range from $149 for two full-length practice tests, 279 practice questions and 429 online flash cards, to $1,399 for a class of four students.

The bottom line: as I said before, it pays to prepare for the exams, but if you can't pay those high costs, give the free software from the GRE site a shot. And check out some of the books on Amazon, such as *GRE 2016 Test Prep Study Guide* by "Test Prep Books," or the iconic *Princeton Review Cracking the GRE* series which are updated annually.

When you do take the exams, as you well know by now (but have no doubt ignored many a time to your chagrin), get plenty of rest the night before, avoid sugar and carbohydrates (they will give you a quick high, then you'll come crashing down), and eat protein. Limit the caffeine; like sugar, it will give you a high, followed by a low if you have too much. Don't drink a whole pot. While taking the test, don't let your mind wander; once it starts drifting, slap those thoughts right out of your head and get back to the task at hand.

If you're worried about finishing the test in time, the American Disabilities Act allows anyone with a diagnosis of Attention Deficit Hyperactivity Disorder (ADHD) to have extra time to take the tests. Personally, I think anyone can walk into a doctor's office and come out with an ADHD diagnosis, just as long as they say they have trouble focusing and can't pay attention for more than a few minutes before becoming distracted.

As far as I know, and I may be wrong, there are no objective, biological tests for ADHD, so you might want to give that approach a shot—but if you do so, you will have a permanent record of having a psychological disorder and that's no way to start a career if you can help it. You may also walk away with a prescription for Ritalin (a chemical clone of cocaine) or Adderall (an amphetamine). Both may give you an edge for the exam, but both may also lead to a terrible addiction that could increase your anxiety, affect your cognitive processes (in a bad way), make you paranoid and do far more damage than good. In fact, if you're already thinking that it might be a good idea to have such meds to improve your performance, you're already making bad decisions. My personal advice is don't go that route no matter what, and if you can't sit still and pay attention for the time it takes to learn something, then get off the damn computer and toss your smart phone into a puddle of mud. I know that others feel strongly otherwise, however, so make your own decision.

Once you've taken the test, if you don't like your scores, you can have them cancelled. You can retake the exams one month later and up to five times per year. But you can't retake just one part of it; if you got a great score on one part and bombed another, you'll have to decide whether to give it another shot or not. When I took the exams, I scored in the 97th percentile in analytical, but a very low 70th percentile in quantitative. One of my professors insisted I retake it when I applied for a Ph.D. program, stating that there was no way my analytical scores could fall. I, being so analytically brilliant, knew better. I was bound to sink that impressive score on the second try, if not because the score had been a mistake, then because I'd shed more brain cells and become all the more impatient in the year since I'd last taken it. So I opted to stick with the crappy quantitative score, and revel in the stellar analytical—a good move, as the analytical score helped me to get into an excellent doctoral program—one that didn't give much thought to how well I could add and subtract. (Because if I had been better at adding and subtracting, I would have figured out what a bad investment a Ph.D. program actually is.)

Just what is a "good score" you might be asking? That's a tough question, but in general, the scores for the verbal and quantitative portions range from 130 to 170. The mean generally falls somewhere around 150, so you want to score higher than that. The analytical portion of the exam is scored from 0-6 in half point increments. You want to aim for at least 4.5, and preferably 5 or more. Focus less on the score itself, than on the percentile. If you were in the 100th percentile, that means 100 percent of the people scored as much or lower than you—in other words, you're the best! If you scored in the 30th percentile, well, we'll get to that. There are still schools that don't require the GRE, and that's pretty much your only option.

Pay close attention to the minimum GRE the schools and departments you are applying to will accept. Often the graduate school has one standard, and the department a higher standard. Be sure you look over their websites (in the section for "future students" or "admission requirements" or some variation of either), to know their bottom line. Sometimes they're more flexible about the bottom line than they state, but often they aren't. Just be clear that you are applying to a program where your scores are within the range of what they're looking for.

THE GMAT

If you are interested in an MBA or a graduate degree in accounting or finance, then you're likely to have to take the Graduate Management Admission Test or GMAT. The GMAT doesn't test for business or management knowledge. Like the GRE's, the GMAT measures verbal, quantitative and analytical abilities, which give the admission committee a (theoretical) sense of your critical reasoning and logic.

The GMAT is similar to the GRE in format. It is a computerized test of just under four hours, and like the GRE is comprised of Analytical, Verbal and Quantitative sections. It has one additional section, however, and that is Integrated Reasoning.

The Analytical section is pretty much like the GRE's; the first essay presents an issue for you to analyze and the second essay presents an argument that you are to analyze. The Verbal section tests your reading comprehension and critical reasoning skills. You will be tested on your ability to distinguish assumptions, hypotheses and evidence, and your grammar will be tested through sentence correction. The Verbal section is 75 minutes. The Quantitative section is comprised of 37 multiple choice questions focusing on problem solving and data analysis, and you'll also have 75 minutes to complete it.

The Integrated Reasoning section is 12 questions that you need to address in 30 minutes. You are presented with four different formats of data—graphics, tables, "multi-source reasoning" (presented in tabbed sections that contain different data), and "two-part analysis" which involves columns and rows and at this point is already too complicated for me to figure out so head to Wikipedia or some other source for a better understanding of the exam. I see a table or chart or graphic and I immediately think of modern art. No business school in the world, outside of the University of Phoenix, would be foolish enough to admit me.

But hopefully, if you want to go to business school, they'll be wise enough to admit you. So plan on taking it. The GMAT is given year round at testing centers, which are usually colleges or private educational testing centers (such as Kaplan). It costs $250 and includes submitting your scores to five schools and $28.50 for each additional one. The scores for the GMAT range from 200 to 800 with most around 400 to 600. The average GMAT score is about 540, so do your best to beat that.

To prepare for the test, your options are pretty much the same as for the GRE. The official site for the GMAT (www.mba.com) offers free test prep software, and the Princeton Review (www.princetonreview.com) provides test prep packages ranging from $150 to $1,099. Veritas Prep has received excellent reviews for their GMAT preparation, but it's pricey—it costs $950 just for online self-paced practice tests, and up to $6,950 for private tutoring. And just as with the GRE, there are a number of GMAT prep books available, including the Princeton Review series, so browse through some of those if you're looking for an affordable, self-directed option.

After you've taken the test, you'll have the opportunity to preview your unofficial score and here's the cruel and twisted part—you have two minutes to decide if you want to keep it or not. Yep, just like a game show. If you choose to cancel the score, you'll have 60 days to change your mind, but that will cost you $100. Just taking the damn test is a test of your good judgment under pressure.

Like the GRE, the GMAT has not been a very good predictor of student success, but there is an entire industry in testing services, so it's likely to be around a good long time. Unfortunately, admissions committees tend to favor the GMAT scores, assuming that there is a correlation between aptitude and attitude, which as you well know, is just not the case (see, already you're showing more sense than a lot of these professors). Bottom line: study for it, and do well, or find a school that doesn't require it (I'll get to that).

As significant as the MBA is to admissions, the good news for many of you is that business schools are often much more interested in a candidate's work experience than most other programs. For that reason, there are many part-time evening MBA programs designed for working students, something many other graduate programs do not offer.

In fact, there are MBA programs in the UK and US that don't even require an undergraduate degree if the candidate has extensive business experience. In addition, there are a number of "Executive MBA" programs from elite schools that are pricey, but can be taken online and part-time, enabling you to graduate with an MBA from a prestigious school, such as MIT's Sloan School of Management offers.

While there was a period following the recession of 2008 when MBA's were not the golden ticket to a job that they once were, and far too many graduates were not finding jobs, that seems to be turning around. Jobs for business analysts who can crunch big data are predicted to be among the fastest growing good-paying jobs into the 2020's, and *Bloomberg Business*[1] predicts rapid growth in hiring MBA's, including from "B-schools," or second best MBA programs.

THE LSAT

Whereas the market for MBA's is promising, the market for law school graduates, unfortunately, is not. More than 80% of law school graduates not only graduate with substantial debt, but only 40% are finding jobs in large firms, and far too many are not finding jobs in law at all. In a recent article in the New York Times[2], the market for law school graduates tanked in 2010, but has only slightly improved since that time. If you want to go to law school, be sure it's something you really want—not something you're thinking of doing because you don't know what else to do or you think you'll make a lot of money. There will always be lawyers who make a ton of money, but they tend to be the ones who really love the law and work really, really hard. Or become divorce attorneys. There's always money to be made in heartbreak.

But if you do want to take a gamble and go to law school, you're going to have to take the Law School Admissions Test, or LSAT.

Unlike the GRE and the GMAT, which are offered throughout the year, the LSAT is only offered four times a year, in February, June, October and December.

There are six sections to the LSAT, but only four are scored. The writing sample is not scored and one of the multiple choice sections is an experimental

1 Kitroeff, Natalie (2015), "MBA's are Graduating Into the Best Job Market in a Decade," *Bloomberg Business,* May 19, available online at: http://www.bloomberg.com/news/articles/2015-05-19/mbas-are-graduating-into-the-best-job-market-in-a-decade

2 Olson, Elizabeth (2015), "Burdened With Debt, Law School Graduates Struggle With Job Market," *New York Times,* April 26

sections to test the questions, but you won't know which one it is. So you're sort of like a critically-ill patient who doesn't know if you're getting the life saving drug or the placebo, but what choice do you have but to go for it?

Unlike the GRE or GMAT, there's actually some evidence that the LSAT is a more accurate predictor of graduate school success, at least in the first year. You absolutely want to do well on the LSAT if you want to get into a good program.

You will have five 35 minute multiple choice sections followed by a writing sample. Only four of the multiple choice sections will be scored. The writing sample is not scored, but will be sent to the law schools you select as an example of your writing and reasoning skills. For that section, you will have 35 minutes to draft a well-reasoned essay based on set of presented facts.

But before drafting your writing sample, you will have two 35-minute sections of Logical Reasoning and each contains 25 multiple choice questions. These questions test your ability to identify main points in an argument, the evidence supporting them, and apply logic to abstract concepts. The Analytical Reasoning section includes 25 multiple choice questions, and you have 35 minutes to complete it. Similar to the Logical Reasoning section, the Analytical Reasoning section tests your ability to understand the implications of rules and relationships between concepts.

Then there's a 35 minute section on Reading Comprehension, which is 27 multiple choice questions designed to test your ability to understand the main and lesser points of text. You will also have one hour for three more Reading Comprehension sections which test your ability to identify themes and main ideas, and comprehend dense and complex text.

Altogether, the LSAT takes about 3 ½ hours and costs $175. There's an additional fee of $170 for Law School Data Assembly Service (LSDAS) which most law schools require. THE LSDAS is actually a convenience, because you submit all your letters of recommendation, personal statement, and test scores directly to them, and they submit them to the law schools directly. If you're late in registering for the LSAT, there's an additional fee of $90. LSAT fees can be waived, however, if you're utterly poor. You need to submit tax forms and fill out a ton of paperwork to prove your indigence, but if you're really broke—and really bright—you might be able to get the fees waived and stand a good shot at scholarships.

The maximum score for the LSAT is 180, and the average score is 150. To learn more, go directly to the Law School Admission Council site (www.lsac. org) where you'll find information on test prep and registering. You can even take a free practice LSAT test from their site. For more costly test prep, there's the usual cast of characters, Princeton Review, which charges from $799 to $1,349 and even higher; Kaplan which charges from $799 to $2,599; plenty of lesser-known sites I know nothing about, and lots of test prep books available through Amazon. As always, I advise going the free or low cost route first, and then if you need more help and can afford it, consider investing in the course format that best suits your learning style, budget and needs.

THE MCAT

Now we've come to the MCAT. The Medical College Admission Test (MCAT) is a grueling test clearly designed to weed out those who can't withstand hours of pressure. It is 7 and a half hours, and includes 230 multiple choice questions with testing on eight different subjects: verbal, biology, general chemistry, organic chemistry, biochemistry, physics, psychology and sociology.

The MCAT focuses on content knowledge, critical thinking, research design and graphical analysis and data interpretation, with the questions designed for you to show how the various sciences relate to medicine. The verbal reasoning section focuses exclusively on the social sciences and humanities, but for the other sections, you will need a basic undergraduate foundation in the sciences. You do not need to have advanced knowledge of any of these subjects, just a basic, introductory knowledge like you would find taking undergraduate courses in those subjects.

Don't skimp on preparing for the verbal portion of the exam. Many medical schools give even more weight to the verbal section than they do the science section, because they believe it is a good indication of your reasoning and critical thinking skills—skills that are essential for anyone who wants to be a physician. Moreover, students with humanities and social science backgrounds tend to test higher on the verbal portion compared to students with degrees in the sciences, so you'll be competing with them. Be prepared!

The total possible points for the MCAT is 578. If you score below 470, you're going to need other strengths to offset the low score, such as a very high GPA, and/or excellent work experience.

According to Princeton Review, about half of the people who take the MCAT retake it, and most who do well put in between 200 and 300 hours of study. If that seems too strenuous, you should probably rethink medical school—it's rigorous, and followed by an even more rigorous internship. The life of a physician may be a rewarding one, but you've got to put in some really hard work to get—and to stay—there.

The American Association of Medical Colleges' website (https://students-residents.aamc.org/) offers a preparation guide for the MCAT which tells more details about the exam and registration process. It is available in ebook or print form for $30, but to get the 120 practice test questions, you need to buy "the bundle" which is $35. As with the other graduate admissions exams, Kaplan, Petersons, and Princeton Review offer a range of prep packages, and there are many books available on Amazon. But test prep for med school (just like the cost of medical textbooks once you make it in) doesn't come cheap. Princeton Review, for example, charges $1,899 for their cheapest self-paced course, up to $9,499 for a class of eight. These courses are only offered in Austin, Orlando and San Diego, so if you don't live there, you'll also have to pay for room and board (offered for an additional fee of several thousand dollars) and airfare. If you're going to med school, get used to it. It won't come cheap.

When you arrive to take the test, you will be "biometrically" registered, which includes being photographed, digitally fingerprinted and subjected to a full body scan, but as far as I know they won't put you in a line-up nor send you off to jail. Medical school will be punishment enough for any possible sins you have committed in your lifetime. Or perhaps this creepy video at https://vimeo.com/74953443 of what to expect, which you can find on the MCAT site, will be punishment enough. (Be sure to watch to the very end, when the speaker turns and walks away, letting her smile collapse into a pout. It's straight out of an SNL skit.) The upside to the biometric registration process, however, is you get to go to the bathroom so what's a little fingerprinting and radiation exposure?

The cost of taking the MCAT, which is offered fifteen times throughout the year, is $305, assuming you register at least one month in advance, up to $355 if you wait until a week before. There is also a fee assistance program for those with demonstrated and extreme financial need; if you qualify, the fee for the MCAT starts at $115, up to $165 for late registration.

BOMBING (OR NOT TAKING) THE EXAMS

So what happens if you bomb the exams or decide not to take them at all? Can you still get into a graduate program? The short answer is yes, you can. The long answer is your options will be significantly more limited.

There are a number of universities or programs in the U.S. that don't require entrance exams. In many cases, a university might require them for most of their programs, but certain departments won't require them. And those that don't are not necessarily inferior schools; because there is such a poor correlation between these test scores and how students do, many excellent and even Ivy League programs don't require them. Columbia, University of California Berkeley, Cornell, MIT, Johns Hopkins, Purdue and many others have graduate programs that do not require entrance exams.

But which ones these are constantly change. Some schools that have required them for years drop the requirement, and others that have not required them for years suddenly require them. Add to that the variation among department requirements where one department requires them and another does not, and the bottom line becomes: check into it at the time of application. I provide you some guidelines, but they're only accurate today, as I write this. By the time you read this book, many of the schools may have required them, while other schools may have dropped the requirement. Be clear when you apply if you need to take the exams or not.

As for the GRE's, Ainsley Diduca's website, (http://ainsleydiduca.com/grad-schools-dont-require-gre/) offers a list of graduate disciplines, and if you click on the link to the discipline you're interested in, it will take you to a list of grad programs that don't require the GRE. Again, check to be sure the information is up to date by going directly to the admissions requirements of the department, but it will at least give you a start.

When it comes to getting an MBA, you may have an even better shot at being able to avoid taking the GMAT, if you have a strong undergraduate education and excellent professional experience. Executive MBA programs are even less likely to require the GMAT—but are more expensive because they are designed for mid-career professionals who usually have a corporation paying their way.

Most European universities, including those in the United Kingdom, do not require the GRE or GMAT, but that is beginning to change, especially when it comes to the GMAT as more prestigious universities require it. There was a time when few Canadian universities required the tests, but it is much more common now, and most of the top Canadian universities require the GRE.

As for the LSAT, that's much tougher. Until 2014, the American Bar Association (ABA) compelled all accredited law schools to require the LSAT. They relaxed that rule a bit in 2014, but only to allow up to 10% of an entering freshman law class to be admitted without taking the LSAT, and of that ten percent, they must have obtained their undergraduate degree from the same law school or be pursuing a dual-degree (such as a JD/Ph.D.). It gets even more tricky, because to be admitted without the LSAT you must have scored in the top 85% of another admissions test, such as the SAT (School Admissions Test, used for undergraduate admissions, or GRE), and must have been in the top 10% of your class for six semesters, or received a minimum GPA of 3.5.

In other words, most law schools require the test, and of those that don't, the rules they have to comply with are so stringent that chances are you'll have to take it.

Since the ABA relaxed the rule, only a few law schools have dropped the requirement (remember, though, you still have to be in the top ten percent of your class and scored in the top 85% of another admissions test). These law schools are Drake University School of Law, University of Iowa Law School, SUNY-Buffalo Law School and St. John's University School of Law.

The Massachusetts School of Law in Andover, Massachusetts does not require the LSAT for anyone, but they are not accredited with the ABA. They are accredited by the New England Association of Schools and Colleges, and have won several awards for their advocacy program, but graduating from an unaccredited law school can significantly limit where you practice, as most states won't admit you to the bar. But by the time you read this, their accreditation status may have changed, as well as their admissions requirements.

Finally, what about medical school? Is there any way to avoid taking that day-long, costly test and still get into med school? Of course there is. A list of several medical schools that do not require it can be found at this website: (http://www.collegeadmissionspartners.com/bsmd-programs/bsmd-programs-dont-require-mcat/) but be sure to check to be sure the program you're interested in hasn't changed the requirement.

So now that we've gotten through all this talk of exams, which is nearly as tedious as the exams themselves, it's time to think about your resume.

Chapter 10

● ● ●

PREPARE YOUR RESUME OR CURRICULUM VITA

Many departments request a resume or CV. Be sure you have one and it is up to date. There are a number of books and online articles you can find about how to write them, so I won't go into too much detail, but a few pointers.

For either a resume or a CV, look first at the header. Delete any markers such as "email:" "phone:" "address:" and that sort of thing. Just put in the email, phone and address. They will know what they are. (Though you can distinguish cell phone and home phone and that sort of thing.)

Make sure your email address is a personal one, not an employer's email. If you have an email address associated with your school, however, the type that ends in .edu, then you can use that.

Put your education upfront. Make it the first thing they see. If you haven't yet finished your undergraduate degree, just list the date you will graduate, with B.A. (or B.S. or M.A. or whatever) candidate. The word candidate makes it clear that you have not yet received the degree, while listing the year makes it clear that you will have it by the time you enter the graduate program.

Be sure to list your university and your major. You can also list a minor, but do not list previous majors or minors if you've changed them.

Typically, for a resume you want to keep it brief, and chances are it is brief because you're probably just starting out your career. But for a CV, the general rule is the longer the better, unless they require a brief one.

A resume will list your education; your work experience; the details of what you did in that work, including responsibilities and achievements; community service; and any awards or recognitions. You will list the most recent degrees, jobs, and awards first.

If you received any scholarships or honors as an undergraduate, list those.

A Curriculum Vita is a document of your scholarly and professional achievements. You will list your degrees, just as in a resume, and your employment, but you will only list your job titles, place of employment, and years of employment. *You will not list what you did in that job in your CV.*

A CV will also list any publications you have had, any public presentations you have given, any awards or honors you've received, and your community service and volunteer work.

You probably won't have the achievements to go the CV route, but if you continue in academia or scholarly work, you will start building it up as soon as you enter graduate school. If you are transferring from a masters to a doctoral program, then you should use a CV, with your thesis (if any) listed as a publication (all theses are technically publications). If it is not yet finished, you simply add the word "forthcoming" with the anticipated date of completion.

In most cases, however, you will have a resume, so be sure it's up to date, professional, and accurate.

Unlike applying for a job, however, potential professors will not be contacting your former employers. You never want to lie on your resume, because if you were admitted to the program and it was discovered you lied on your application, you could get kicked out. But if you were fired from a job or had a boss who'd trash you, go ahead and list the job. They won't investigate your past.

Except that some will type your name into a search engine and see what comes up, which is where you might not want them going.

Chapter 11

● ● ●

GOOGLE YOURSELF

Alright, you've sent in all your application materials, including a brilliant Personal Statement and an impressive resume or CV, even if it demonstrates that you have limited experience, but you're ready to launch your professional career. Your references are stellar, or at the very least, acceptable, you've done your homework on the universities and departments you're applying to and reached out to several faculty.

Then, just when you've thoroughly impressed them, one or more faculty members does just what any potential employer is going to do. They Google you. They see what's online, take a look at your Facebook page, checked to see if you have any Twitter and Linked In accounts. They may even look for any YouTube, Instagram, or Tinder accounts you might have. Why are they doing this? Maybe you so wowed them they're expecting to find all sorts of impressive accomplishments on the internet. Maybe they want to check out the credibility of your claims. Or maybe they just want to see how stupid you really are and whether admitting you will ultimately embarrass them. (And maybe they just want to get into bed with you, and they're total creeps.)

To the extent you can delete anything, delete any photos depicting nudity or partial nudity or outfits fit only for strippers or drug dealers, whether on you or on your friends. Don't start moralizing about "slut shaming" and the like. Just get it off there and keep it off there if you want to come across as serious and professional.

Delete anything and everything that is intended to tease, put down or smear another person or group of people, no matter who they are.

Be extremely judicious about political expressions. It's perfectly fine to express your political opinions on line, but how do those opinions correspond to the political sensibilities of the department and/or faculty you're applying to work with?

Unless you're applying for graduate studies in human sexuality, it's best to delete any and all references to sex, except for the most benign, which is to say, something that would bring a smile to your grandmother's face. Unless of course, your grandmother is Dr. Ruth and sex is all she talks about, in which case, forget about the advice not to include your grandparents in your personal statement, and go for it! Tell the faculty you grew up in the land of the weird and the home of the whacky and now you've rebelled by being discrete.

Delete all those photos of you "partying" or boasting about getting drunk or high. Similarly, delete all references that boast of drug use. Advocating for the legalization of marijuana is one thing. Bragging about how stoned you got at some wild party is another.

Delete rants and rage. Anything that comes across as uncontrolled rage, long-standing anger at wrongs done to you, or attacks on others will work against you. No one wants to be around an angry person, even if that anger is understandable and justified. Similarly, delete anything that blames others for your failures. Aim for an image of maturity and responsibility, not the next Donald Trump.

Finally, check your privacy settings and be sure as much content as possible is not accessible to the public.

Once you've done all that, stick to it. For the rest of your life, use your social media presence to promote yourself, not embarrass or exclude you. You're growing up now, and the best way to have fun is to know your fun won't become a public topic. (I knew one graduate student who put a photo of one of her professors on her Facebook page with comments about the crush she had on him—you can imagine how quickly that got back to him! He kept his distance after that.)

And the same goes for those tattoos. Sure, most students and now even half the professors have illustrated their flesh for all to see. Some tattoos are quite impressive, but some others not so much. Even if you're admitted to the department with a full-ride scholarship and honors, once they see you've tattooed "Stoner" on your forehead or a bug-eyed zombie on your cleavage, you're doomed. Cover up any tattoos that scream, "I'm not that bright," unless that's how you want the world to view you.

Now, assuming you do get in, just how in the world are you going to pay for it?

Chapter 12

● ● ●

GET PAID TO GO TO SCHOOL

The university that accepts you may be thinking of you as a consumer, but the faculty who work with you—as well as your graduate student colleagues— are thinking of you as a professional. Graduate school is your profession, at least for now, so begin thinking of your education not as "still in school," but as the early legs of your career.

And that means getting paid to do it, rather than paying for it. There is a great deal of competition among graduate students for funding, so unless you have outstanding GRE scores, an excellent GPA and impressive experience, you may well need to beg, borrow or steal during your first semester or year, or even through your entire grad school career. But that doesn't mean you can't get funding; it just means you need to know where to look.

First, *be sure when you apply that you mark the section on the application that asks if you need funding.* But you can't stop there. They will only tell you about a portion of the funds, the assistantships and a few internal scholarships. But there's much more out there, though it is limited and competitive. So *be sure that you let everyone you speak to in the department and university know that you need funding.* Many people who would otherwise have qualified for fund-ing opportunities are passed over because they overlooked this detail. Some people think that funding is a form of charity, and they would rather work for it. But it is not by any means charity.

There are really only two kinds of funding, not counting college loans. You either receive a work opportunity, such as a research assistant or teaching assistant position, or you receive an award. Even a "needs based" award—granted on the basis of financial need—is an honor, because these are competitive awards. Not everyone who needs funding gets it, but those who are determined to get funding usually figure out how to get it.

The advantages to graduate assistantships are significant. The most important advantage is that in almost all cases, tuition and fees are waived. The pay might be paltry, but just having the tuition and fees waived, particularly if you are paying out-of-state tuition, is significant.

The second advantage is that you do receive some salary, and increasingly, health insurance and other benefits. The pay may be as little as $500 a month for "quarter time" assistantships (about ten hours a week, in theory) to $1,000 or even $1,500 a month for half or full-time assistantships. The pay varies by university, and as university budgets are cut, they may become the first target of the budgetary hatchet, but there is usually always a salary that comes with a graduate assistantship.

The third advantage to a graduate assistantship is that it provides invaluable experience and an opportunity to work closely with faculty. A teaching assistantship can include anything from helping a professor grade papers to actually teaching a course. A research assistantship can include anything from doing absolutely nothing to working side by side with a professor on an important research project and in many cases even publishing.

The downside to graduate assistantships is that you may have to work long hours on top of your regular coursework. Although there is supposed to be a cap on the hours you work, it is very common that quarter-time graduate assistants work half or full time, and half-time assistants work full time. They can become exploited and some faculty treat their grad assistants like sweatshop workers (though most faculty are very sensitive to the exploitation of graduate students and treat their assistants with respect, advocate for better pay and benefits and caps on their time).

You may also find yourself working for an instructor, which is especially common in research universities. In these cases the instructor may be part time or full time, good at what they do or bad at what they do, but in every case, underpaid and overworked. These teaching assistant positions typically include grading papers and preparing Power Point presentations and even writing exams. The class size is typically the size of a small town, and you are often one of several grad students assisting the class. If you get one of these positions, you will work hard, but so will the instructor you are reporting to. Be sure to treat him or her with as much respect as you'd treat a professor because they do gossip, they are probably treated like crap by the faculty, and they will likely reward you by letting you give lectures on occasion, which is excellent experience whatever career you go into. After all, there's no better way to master public speaking than by teaching a class, and almost all professions require some form of public speaking at one point or another.

The bottom line is, if you get a teaching or research assistant position you can be exploited, and you probably will be, but the experience can be invaluable. (And even if you find yourself doing nothing or stuffing envelopes or some such thing, at least "it looks good on paper" once you call it "marketing and public relations.") So by all means, try to get a graduate assistantship if you can, and try to hold on to it once you get it.

Other forms of funding are grants and scholarships, and they can be needs-based, merit-based, interest-based or membership-based. Weird as some of these grants are, you may be surprised to find some pots of money you are eligible for. They are usually small pots, but you can cobble together a pretty good chunk of change with enough of them. Cobbling is an all-important but much overlooked survival strategy in graduate school, and more on that later. But first, let's take a look at the "certain kinds of people" pots of gold that you just might not know about.

For fun, Google "weird scholarships." This should keep you entertained for an hour or so, and may even get you some money. The Zombie Apocalypse Scholarship could land you $1,000 if you can devise a plan on where to hide in the event of a zombie apocalypse. Really. The Eileen J. Garrett scholarship funds studies in the paranormal, if that's your thing. Scholarships are granted to people who study anything related to knitting, people who wear milk mustaches, people who can skateboard, and even people who excel at duck calling (though it won't help you with grad school; it's strictly limited to high school seniors who are just getting started in their duck calling careers).

But more commonly, and less weirdly, are the scholarships for people who belong to a certain group (like the Daughters of the American Revolution or the Girl Scouts of America), or work or have a relative who works for a specific corporation. If you work for a corporation, be sure to see if they have any funds for graduate school—even if it's not in your favored field of study, it might be enough to get you started and you can transfer to the program you prefer later on. And if your parents or spouse works for a corporation, see if their employers have a tuition program that extends to dependents or relatives. There are grants for single parents, and grants for children of single parents. Talbot's clothing store provides an annual scholarship of up to $10,000 for women returning to school, and scholarships based on race, gender, or national origin or heritage are common. But you do not have to be a member of a "minority" group to get funded; remember, there are many grants available to people based on a multitude of factors; you just need to know where to find them.

In addition to the lazy route of Googling, you should always go to your local and university libraries and ask to speak to the librarian in charge of grants and scholarships. Librarians may be the last group on earth who actually love to help other people and it's well worth your trouble getting to know them. Explain that you want to find all possible sources of grants and scholarships to fund your education, and ask what resources are available. There should be a wealth of information available to guide you on your search, and your librarian will in all likelihood be delighted to help you. If not, or after spending an hour together you walk away with no better idea than the confusion you walked in with, find another librarian or another library altogether.

Grants and scholarships will come from the federal government, corporations, private individuals, professional organizations and associations, and your university. In addition to what you find from the grants librarian, *you will also want to contact people in the following units of the university you are applying to: the department and any faculty who have grants; the college or dean's office; the graduate school; and the research institutes and centers at the university.*

This last source, the research institutes and centers, can be invaluable. They usually have funding for one or more graduate students each semester, and some students have their entire graduate career paid for by landing a job or grant from one of these places. Look up the Director or whoever is in charge, and contact them directly—but as you've already figured out by now, before you contact them, look up what and where they teach, and what their research interests are. In almost all cases, they will have a joint appointment with an academic department, which may or may not be the one that you are applying to. If it's not the same, that doesn't matter, as long as what you are applying to relates in some way to the center. Just be sure you know something about the center and the person you'll be contacting. The more you can show an interest in their work, the more likely they'll show an interest in yours.

No matter what you find out when you contact each of these sources for funding opportunities, *always ask if they have any other suggestions for where you might look.* Even if they have funding available, it does not hurt to ask about other sources in the event you aren't selected (though if they appear to be favoring you, it might be best not to present yourself as so eager for more places to look that you come across as hoping for something better; be judicious). But never leave empty-handed without at least asking if they know of anyplace else you should check out.

If they have nothing for you, thank them and follow up with a thank you email asking to be kept in mind if anything does come up. Then follow up at the end of the semester. (If they have something for you, or the possibility of something, also be sure to follow up with a thank you, and be sure you know if there is any formal application you need to fill out. And be sure to follow up, in case you are forgotten or brushed to the side.)

Remember, *decisions are made for funding early on*—sometimes as much as a year in advance, though usually more like a semester in advance. But—and this is very important—*budgets are often finalized at the last minute,* funded students leave or find other opportunities at the last minute, or someone gets an unexpected grant or even discovers they have to spend some money quickly. There is also time at the end of the academic year when a department or unit has to spend any money it hasn't yet spent or lose it—*so there's money to give away.* What this means is that *there are always last minute opportunities that become available,* so making sure that people know your name and who you are and that you need money and are available, will put you in the front of the line for these last-minute good fortunes.

Federal grants can also be very lucrative. The U.S. Department of Education's Foreign Language and Area Studies (FLAS) scholarship is a very attractive scholarship for students who want to conduct research in developing countries and must learn a foreign language. It funds tuition, fees, travel and provides a generous stipend ($18,000 as of 2016). You can find out more about it through the FLAS coordinator at the international centers and graduate school or the university you plan to attend, assuming you are going to a large university (it may not be available at smaller colleges).

Fulbright awards are very prestigious and not as difficult to get as many other graduate scholarships, such as the National Science Foundation Dissertation Improvement Award or the Social Science Research Council awards. Don't assume that you can't get one; even if your undergraduate grades were low, you might discover that after a year in graduate school, the support of your professors, and a decent research project, you are very competitive for these awards. If you are finishing up your undergrad, ask about Fulbrights at your college; you just may qualify for one to get started in your first year of graduate school (and if you are going into the STEM field or social sciences, ask about National Science Foundation awards, and NASA awards). If the first person you speak to doesn't know the answer, keep asking. But if you are still in college and applying for graduate school, you are already in an excellent place to find out what is available when you graduate. If you are already out of college, there is always a university nearby or the university you are applying to, that can help you out.

Always remember that just because you don't get a scholarship or award one year, it does not mean that you cannot try again the next—or even the following semester. I applied for a Fulbright one year, did not get it, and reapplied the following year. In the meantime, I was all set to get started on my doctoral dissertation which required travel to another country where I would live for a year. But without the Fulbright, I had no money to go.

So I presented my needs to the research centers throughout my university. Doing that required nothing more than a phone call, an email, or at most, a one-page letter that included the cost of my airfare, living expenses, and reason for going. No one had any official "grant money," but they had discretionary funds that they could use to support an academic project.

I received enough little pots of money—five hundred here, a thousand there, maybe even only one hundred dollars from some—that I was able to buy my airfare and get to my research site. Just before I left I got word that I'd been awarded a grant from the National Science Foundation, and shortly after getting to the field site, received word that I'd been awarded the Fulbright this time around.

What does that mean for you? It means, *don't give up when you are rejected, which you will be. Keep applying,* let people know you need the money, and proceed toward your goals in the meantime.

Most of the major research grants will go to doctoral students, so if you are only in it for the Master's, which is probably the most sensible ambition, the funding available to you will be in the form of graduate assistantships and little pots of money (which often fund travel, research or attending professional meetings).

But there's a trick to becoming eligible for those doctoral grants—don't apply for the terminal Master's. Apply for the Ph.D. program and pick up your Master's after two years. Here's how it works. You apply for the doctoral program, gushing about how you want to pursue an academic or government/non-profit career or, if applicable, go into clinical work (as in getting your doctorate in psychology, for example, where such work exists in contrast to a doctorate in sociology, where such work does not exist).

Students who aren't doing well in doctoral programs are usually encouraged to get out after a couple of years and handed the Master's as a courtesy, though in most cases it requires writing a short thesis or taking some exams. Students who decide a couple of years in that the doctorate isn't for them usually opt for applying for the Master's before they go, if they have any sense at all.

There's no reason you can't take that same route, and here are the advantages of doing so. You will get more faculty attention. You will be eligible for more funding. And if you aren't able to get a job in your field but owe student loans or don't want to have any stretches of unemployment on your career history, you could continue on beyond the Master's since you'd already be in a doctoral program.

Now for the disadvantages, and they're big. It will be harder to get into a doctoral program than a terminal Masters if you have low scores, a low GPA or an otherwise weak record. If you do opt out after a couple of years, even if that was your intent all along, then no matter how much the faculty like you, they will see you as someone who quit. They may well understand why you did so, but you will be perceived as having dropped out of the doctoral program, rather than having completed the Master's program, even if you do walk away with the Master's degree. And those faculty will likely be the very people you will need to write your letters of recommendation when you hit the job market.

So that route is probably not the best way to go, but it is an option.

On the other hand, if you are in a doctoral program and are serious about pursuing the doctorate, *be sure you take a course in research design as soon as possible.* If your department, or none of the departments in your college, offers such a course, find a professor who has a good track record of grants and ask to take an independent study in research design under their supervision. Your goal should be to produce a fundable grant proposal by the end of the course, which hopefully includes developing your research agenda and designing a research project to get started on. *Knowing how to write a grant proposal means knowing how to get money to fund your education and research projects.* It also gives you a useful skill once you hit the job market. So if you're going to be in graduate school for more than a couple of years, take a course in research design.

Chapter 13

●　●　●

A WORD ABOUT STUDENT LOANS

If you have no other option, a loan for the first semester and even the first year can be sensible. But *do not plan on funding your entire education on loans*, especially if you are not in a program that will assure you of a decent shot at a job when you finish. Students who come out of school fifty to a hundred grand or more in debt and no more employable—and in some cases less employable—than before they went in, are setting themselves up for a future of indentured servitude. *Don't take out a loan just because you qualify!* Only take out a loan because you have no other choice. If someone tells you a student loan is a great way to finance a car, think again. By the time you finish grad school, that car won't be worth much, while your loan payments will have only just begun. I've known students who have taken out student loans they didn't need just to buy new clothes, take vacations, or eat at expensive restaurants, boasting that it's a wise financial move because it "builds up their credit score," or is far less interest than a credit card. Newsflash: getting credit in America is easy. You don't need to go into debt to get it. And yes, the interest rate is less than a credit card, but paying for such a lifestyle two or more years after you've enjoyed the pricey frills is a real drag. And for many of the loans you'll be accruing interest during those years, so don't think you're saving money. Most student loans are not subsidized. The rate on private loans can be as high as 20%, depending on your credit. In other words, student loans are not as cheap as you might think.

As for repayment, Sallie Mae, the friendly name they've given the student loan sharks, even has a collection unit just for collecting from prisoners. They will go after you. And if you default, your wages and income tax returns will be garnished. Think of student loans like those flotation devices on airplanes. You don't want to have to use them, but if you need them, know that they are there.

So what's out there? There are two basic types of student loans: federal and private. Interest rates on federal loans is regulated by law, and usually doesn't come to more than 8%, and often is closer to 5%. Private loans are not regulated beyond general credit law, which is to say, you can pay through the roof in interest.

Federal student loans include subsidized and unsubsidized loans. Subsidized loans are loans whose interest is paid by the government while you are in school. Six months after graduating or dropping out (for whatever reason, even if it's just to take a break or recover from an illness) you will start paying back the loan and interest—the government will no longer subsidize it. Stafford loans are federal loans, but not all of them are subsidized. Be sure you are clear before accepting any loan that you know whether or not the loan is subsidized. An unsubsidized loan can easily lead to discovering that for every $100 you repay, only about $30 of it goes to principal and the rest is interest. And the longer you take to repay it, the more interest and less principal you'll be paying.

Perkins loans are needs-based federal loans which are subsidized, and the interest rate is capped at 5% and there is a nine month, rather than six month, grace period between the time you graduate (or quit) and the first payment is due. The maximum amount you can take out for graduate school currently (as of 2016) is $8,000 a year up to a maximum debt load of $60,000 including undergraduate loans. Perkins loans are among the best loans you can take out, and also have the advantage of being cancelled if you go into one of several careers serving under-served populations. These careers include teaching, fire fighting, law enforcement, nursing, speech therapy, Peace Corps, AmeriCorps, and some active-duty postings in the military. Loan cancellation isn't the golden egg it appears to be, however. You must first make 120 on-time minimum payments *for at least ten years,* and prove you are work-ing in one of the eligible professions and serving an under-served population before your loan will be forgiven.

Moreover, if you have been convicted of any drug offenses, you cannot take out a federal loan, subsidized or unsubsidized. You can be a convicted murderer, rapist or embezzler, and you are still eligible for federal loans. But if you got busted for a joint at some rock concert back in your freshman year, forget about it. You must also be a U.S. citizen or an eligible non-citizen with a Social Security number, maintain good grades, and if male and between the ages of 18 and 25, be registered with Selective Service.

Private loans are virtually always unsubsidized and that means that just like unsubsidized federal loans, the minute you accept the loan your interest begins to accrue—on a daily basis. By the time you graduate, that interest can be substantial—and it will continue to accrue as long as you are repaying the loan, which may well be another decade. Private loans are loans that come directly from the college or university, banks, credit unions or other financial institutions. These are the most costly loans—in almost all cases *it is better not to go to graduate school than to go to graduate school on commercial private loans.*

Finally, one last word of caution; too many students want to live a com-fortable middle-class lifestyle while they go to college. If you have a spouse or parents who can enable you to do that, great. But chances are you don't. *If you really want to live a comfortable middle-class lifestyle, then live frugally through college and grad school.* If you do, your chances of prospering once you get out are far greater and that new salary will go to paying for your new lifestyle—not repaying your old one.

CONCLUSION

(OR IF YOU WERE ABLE TO READ THIS FAR AND YOU HAVE AN

UNDERGRAD DEGREE, YOU CAN GET INTO GRAD SCHOOL)

If you've come this far, you've got what it takes to get into grad school. You are willing to take the time to find out what you need to do, you are sufficiently serious about the idea of getting a graduate education that you've just read through nearly a hundred pages of advice. Or at the very least, you've skipped straight to the conclusion which alone is evidence you're ready for the big leagues. After all, most professors only read the abstracts, conclusions and skim a few sub-titles of half of what they "read."

No matter what strikes you have going against you, if you really want to get a graduate education, you can make it happen. It may take a little extra time and effort, but you can get in. And if you don't have too many strikes against you and you have maintained a decent GPA, scored well on your GRE's and have a few good professional contacts, all the better. Now it's just a matter of jumping through the hoops, remaining tenacious and mastering the game.

How well you do once you get in, however, is another matter altogether. But it really doesn't take much more than determination, a bit of social savvy, and not dropping out to get that graduate degree. But first, get in. Get into the best department that you can, under the mentorship of the best and most humane professors, and with funding if at all possible.

Finally, remember that graduate school is not for everyone and it's almost always overrated. Don't jump into it without giving careful thought to what you hope to get out of it. Particularly in the case of doctoral studies, keep in mind that you will be out of the mainstream job market for the length of time it takes to get your degree, while others are accumulating experience and raises. Will you get back the value that you lose by being in school for years? Sometimes, you will, and there is value in an education that cannot be measured by a paycheck. But a paycheck does count, and the lines of the unemployed with dog-eared graduate degrees are long ones. So give it careful thought.

But do keep in mind that a graduate education can be worth every bit of effort and every dollar invested if you choose wisely, explore your options and take advantage of as many opportunities as possible—and approach your education as the entry years to a rewarding career. If you know what you're after and it includes a graduate degree, go for it!

How do you get started? With just one step: just see what's out there. See what possible degrees you might pursue to reach your dreams, and you never know what future might await you.

Appendix I

● ● ●

COMMON PROBLEMS AND SOLUTIONS

Low GPA? Aim for a regional school; you can transfer to a better one after you get your Master's. Did you do better at the end of your degree, such as the last year or two? Then point that out in your letter. Did you start out well and then decline? Explain you had a family tragedy, worked full time or battled a serious illness. Still not meeting the standards? Ask for a probationary period, or sign up to take some graduate classes as a post-baccalaureate student to boost your GPA. Be sure to see which classes, if any, can be counted toward your Master's if and when you do get in.

Low GRE's? In some cases, a good GPA and/or impressive experience will compensate, particularly in disciplines that are not heavily quantitative or based in the sciences. Otherwise, re-take them or aim for a program that doesn't require them. Michigan State University, University of Hawaii, University of Vermont, and Johns Hopkins are just a few of the schools that don't require them, or have programs that don't require them. Be sure you check to see what they post on their website, though, because a school that doesn't require them one year, might require them the next, and many schools require them for some programs but not for others. Or go to Canada or even Europe, where GRE's may not be required at all.

No References? Consider everyone you know reasonably well who can attest to your character, work history, or studies. If you haven't spoken to them in years and they are unlikely to remember you, however, it's better to find someone recent. Volunteer with an organization or community group or individual for a few months and then ask them—but be sure you do excellent work. And if all else fails, fake the letters. As long as they aren't coming from universities, you probably won't get caught. (If you do, hang your head in shame and disappear; apply elsewhere another year with real ones in hand.)

No money? Review Chapter Twelve, take out a student loan if you must, sell your car and take the bus, get a job. But the most logical and effective strategy is to get funded by the university or land an external grant, so read the section on funding carefully and start exploring those options. Money is out there, go get it.

You want to get a graduate degree in a completely different subject than you studied as an undergrad? If your undergraduate degree is in a discipline that is closely related to the discipline you want to study in graduate school, it may not be an issue, particularly if you've had undergraduate courses in that discipline. In most cases you'll be required to take a few introductory undergrad courses in addition to the graduate work, however. But if what you studied as an undergrad is completely unrelated, here's what you need to do: take two years as an undergrad in that discipline, and get a second undergraduate degree. It won't take the full four years because you'll have plenty of prerequisites from your first undergrad degree. If your ultimate aim is a doctorate, you really wouldn't be spending any more time getting a second undergrad degree than if you went into a Master's program at a regional university and then switched to a doctoral program elsewhere. The advantages are that you can boost your GPA, your knowledge of the subject matter will be fresh, and you'll discover—at the undergrad tuition rate which is lower—whether or not the discipline really is the right one for you.

Not enough time to study and take classes? That may change by the time you get admitted. If it doesn't, consider quitting your job if it's a dead end one and you get funding to go to school. Talk with your family about pitching in more around the house. Take just one course per semester if that's all you have time for; it will at least get you moving toward the degree. Take an online course or two if you must, but no more than that. As I've explained earlier, most online degrees are considered a joke by most people and are often far more expensive than traditional degrees. In an earlier era, these were called mail-order degrees. You'll make a better investment with a mail-order bride. If you really cannot find the time to go to graduate school, you probably don't need to go to graduate school because your life is already pretty full. But if you want to go, just put the gears in motion to make it happen and you'll find the time.

You're late in the game and have missed most deadlines but still want to try for admission as soon as possible? Look for schools with "rolling admissions" policies or which accept January admission. Rolling admission means they will accept applications at any time up to the start of the fall semester. The downside is, they may have already filled the class and not be accepting more students. They may also have less status, and need all the grad students they can get. That does not necessarily mean you'd have a poor education. Regional state schools often have rolling admissions and excellent faculty, but they are less specialized (with faculty reflecting a range of expertise) and don't offer doctoral programs, but can provide you the education and degree you're seeking.

The only downside to schools accepting January admissions is you might not bond right away with the grad students who entered in the fall, but if you're friendly and intellectually engaged, you can soon fit in.

Invited for an interview after the application was submitted? That's a good sign. It means you made the first cut. Be prepared for the conversation. Know who the faculty are, what they specialize in and any major publications. Know the university resources, such as research centers and institutions where you might want to participate. Listen, don't babble. If the interview is in person or via Skype, be dressed professionally, but not over-the-top. Think casual professional. Make sure you have good lighting and look around where you'll be seated to see what they'll see behind your head. Make sure it's clean and neat. Be prepared with questions you want the answers to, or in the event they ask if you have any questions. Ask about what courses they will be offering in the next two years, what direction the department is going in (in five years, if you're applying to a doctoral program, next two years if a masters). They'll probably give you about 15 minutes, some less, some up to half an hour. Follow up with a thank you email the following day or a hand-written thank you note mailed the same or following day.

Have a criminal conviction or prison record? Increasingly, universities ask about such convictions, making it all the more difficult to turn your life around. If there is nothing on the application process asking about a criminal record, don't bring it up, unless you're a famous felon. If there is such a question on the application, you must address it. Don't say you were innocent if you weren't (and even if you were, they probably won't believe you). Talk about the education you received in prison, the books you read, and your determination to turn your life around. Focus on the future, not the past.

Worried about writing a thesis? A thesis is just an article, really, and a dissertation is just a series of articles. Don't worry, just take it one step at a time and you'll get it done. And many programs don't require them.

Intimidated at the thought of graduate school? Afraid you might not be grad material? Don't overestimate graduate school. There are some real dumb bunnies there, and they seem to hang on. Besides, once you get in you will quickly catch on and pretty soon you will discover that grad school has taught you to write better, do better research, communicate and debate better and even to think better. After a few weeks it won't be so intimidating after all. Remember, you were once intimidated by Kindergarten, and you got through that. Grad school is just another step along the way.

Appendix II

● ● ●

INTERNATIONAL STUDENTS

First, if you're an international student and you've come straight to this section, be sure to read the book in its entirety. Virtually everything I've written applies to you, but here are some additional things you should know.

I've worked with students from China, Japan, Saudi Arabia, South Korea, South America, Africa and throughout Europe, helping them select, apply for, and gain admission to a variety of graduate programs. They have been admitted to Columbia, MIT, Berkeley and a number of excellent state universities. While I am far from an expert on international students, a few things about international student expectations have struck me.

Many international students are under the impression that only the Ivy Leagues matter. Getting into an Ivy League school is considered an expected achievement for many, and not getting into an Ivy League school is considered a great defeat. If this is your own view, please rethink it. Gaining entry to Ivy League schools is exceptionally difficult and requires a variety of demonstrated achievement, from high entrance exam scores, to outstanding letters of recommendation and a particularly interesting personal statement. Yet as Julie Posselt found in her research of graduate admissions in elite universities[3], because international students work so hard to study for the exams, and in

---

3 Posselt, Julie R. (2016) *Inside Graduate Admissions: Merit, Diversity, and Faculty Gatekeeping*, Cambridge and London: Harvard University Press.

some cases, hire others to take the exams for them, high entrance exams are the norm.

In many cases, only if an international student has a particularly low entrance exam score is it noted; in other words, if you have a score in the 90th percentile and above, that doesn't stand out for an international student. You'll need more evidence of achievement. If you have average to low scores, however, it could screen you out—even if your scores are higher than a domestic student who would be admitted.

Because there is such a pervasive industry in forging transcripts, test scores and letters of recommendation in some countries, international students may have to demonstrate their fit for a university in other ways. Often the letters of recommendation are brief and perfunctory, saying little about a student's achievements, and focusing more on their moral character. When you ask for a letter of recommendation, do your best to encourage the writer recommending you to speak to your academic and professional achievements. The more details the referee (the person writing the letter) can provide about what you have achieved in your education and any research, professional work or community service you have done, the better.

A tendency I have noted in many international students who consult with me is that they are reluctant to discuss problems they have faced and overcome in their life, their family backgrounds, and personal information. If you feel the same way, I know it may be difficult, but the more you can show that you have had adverse or unhappy experiences in your life, but overcome them (or adjusted to them), the better. Faculty like to see that a potential student has the maturity that comes from hardships, the ability to adjust to stress and misfortune, and the strength to grow from these experiences.

One student I worked with adamantly insisted that she had never had a bad experience in her life, and had never known misfortune or adversity. When I urged her to include an example of how she had faced and overcome an obstacle during her education, she wrote that she had once had a rash which embarrassed her. That type of "misfortune" is not something to write about—other applicants have suffered and overcome cancers, paralysis, blindness and other horrific health concerns. Moreover, to write about something as commonplace as a skin rash makes the writer sound like they would complain about the slightest problem. Do not be afraid to discuss poverty, injuries, serious illnesses, setbacks and even failures. But be sure to show how these experiences made you the person you are today, and taught you important lessons in life.

I once worked with a student from China who was bright and creative, but she was unwilling to discuss her family background because she felt that her application should be about her, and not her parents. Of course you can omit your family background if that is your choice, but please understand that the faculty want to know you and your background. A few lines about your family background can give them a much better understanding of who you are, where you came from, and what support you've had to get there. If your family has never been to college, you can show how hard you have worked to become the first in your family to go to college. If your family runs a successful business, you can show how from an early age you were exposed to hard work, an entrepreneurial spirit, and the importance of maintaining strong relationships with clients and workers. If your family has suffered hardships and poverty, you can show how you have overcome these obstacles to reach the place you are at today. And if your family are respected intellectuals, government officials or educators, you can show how your family background has prepared you for academia. In other words, whatever your family background, it has made you the person you are today. You do not need to say much about your family, but two or three lines can make a huge difference in helping the faculty to know you better and want you joining them.

Because international students are not eligible for most state or federal financial aid, and because universities love the higher tuition money international students are charged, if you are able to pay for your education and do not need aid, be sure to say so in your personal statement. Say that you have the assets to fund your education and will not need financial aid, although (if you are applying for a doctoral program), add that you would, of course, pursue and apply for any external research funds. That means that you can pay your way, but you also know that in a doctoral program, the ability to secure grants is important for career success and you would apply for any outside grants you are eligible to apply for.

You will also need to take the TOEFL (Test of English as a Foreign Language) exam, (www.ets.org/toefl) unless your undergraduate degree is from an English-speaking university. Be sure you study for it, and be sure you take it yourself. Julie Posselt found that while entrance exam scores for international students are generally very high, perfect or near perfect entrance exam or TOEFL scores are a red flag that they may have been faked. Moreover, if you do fake your scores and gain admission to an English-speaking university, you could find that you are in way over your head and unable to understand a thing (believe me, I know; I was admitted to a graduate program in France and although I have a basic knowledge of the language and can (or could back then) read French, once I was in the program, I could read the books, but the lectures and discussions were impossible to follow).

No matter how well you do on the TOEFL, you are also likely to be asked for an online interview, such as via Skype. When you have the interview, be ready to ask questions about the department. Simply being agreeable and friendly is not enough; you need to be a bit more assertive than you may be used to when speaking with professors. In America, the student who asks questions about the classes that will be taught, the direction the department is heading, the research institutes or centers at the school, and otherwise shows a knowledge of the faculty expertise, will be the student who stands out.

Finally, back to what I said about reconsidering the elite schools, such as Ivy Leagues. If you are fluent in English, have outstanding test scores, a strong GPA, and even stronger intellect, by all means, do apply to the best schools (and also a few state schools, just in case). But if you lack any of these qualities, don't be discouraged. There are a number of excellent state schools that would welcome you and provide you with a very good, if not outstanding, education. In some cases, the discipline you want to study may include top-rated programs at state universities. Remember, it is the department's status and ranking that you want to look at if you are seeking the best education. Yes, a degree from Stanford in anything will likely secure you a well-paying job. But according to this ranking of Ph.D. programs in physics (http://www. phds.org/rankings/physics), Michigan State University is more highly ranked than Stanford's program. The ranking of the department might show you that a state school offers a better education in your field—and has the reputation for doing so—than the Ivy Leagues. Look at the resources available at the university and the faculty to see if that might be the case in your own discipline of interest.

I know for many of you, however, that your family may not care at all what those program rankings are, or how good a state school is. They expect you to go to the Ivy Leagues. But what if you can't get in? Do you just accept that you have disappointed your family and failed? No. You consider going to a Masters program in one of the public schools in America (or Canada), where you will strengthen your English language skills, establish valuable relationships with faculty in your discipline, gain invaluable research experience in your field, and boost your GPA. Then, after two years, you will apply for a doctoral program to one of the Ivy Leagues, and this time, you very well might get in. And if not, at least you will return to your home country, or stay in the U.S., with a graduate degree from a respected American university.

So, in a nutshell, if you are an international student, do not cheat on your application materials, do not be discouraged if you don't get into the Ivy Leagues, do not be afraid to discuss your personal background and problems you've faced and overcome, and do not be afraid to ask the faculty questions about the program. But do be sure your application essays and materials are reviewed and edited by a native English speaker before submitting them.

One last word of caution, which may not even apply to you. Whatever you do, if you are a male from a country that does not respect female professionals, set those views aside when speaking to female faculty and administrators. Coming to a new country means learning and respecting their culture. Just as you would expect any American coming to your country to respect your cultural traditions and practices, in the United States and most parts of the world, women do supervise, teach, mentor and interact with male students and employees. So don't blow your chances by treating female faculty any differently than male faculty, because they'll notice it and vote against you every time.

Appendix III

● ● ●

RESOURCES

ENTRANCE EXAMS

Educational Testing Service. ETS is a non-profit organization that provides educational testing services. These are the folks who administer the GRE. http://www.ets.org/gre

Law School Admisstion Test. The LSAD is administered by the Law School Admissions Council. http://www.lsac.org

The Graduate Management Admissions Test. The GMAT is needed for entrance into most MBA (Masters of Business Administration) programs and is administered by the Graduate Management Admission Council. Their official site can be found at: http://www.mba.com

The Medical College Admissions Test. The MCAT is administered by the Association of American Medical Colleges. https://www.students-residents.aamc.org

Medical Schools that do not require the MCAT: To find a list of med schools that do not require the MCAT, go to www.collegeadmissions.com. If you can't find it directly, here's the entire link: http://www.collegeadmission-spartners.com/bsmd-programs/bsmd-programs-dont-require-mcat/

TEST PREP

<u>Free Power Prep Software</u> for GRE is available from Educational Testing Service (www.ets.org/gre) : http://www.ets.org/gre/revised_general/prepare/powerprep2

<u>Affordable ($20) software</u> for GRE pre is available at this website: https://www.dxrgroup.com/cgi-bin/scoreitnow/index.pl

<u>Kaplan's</u> offers test prep for the GRE, LSAT, GMAT, and MCAT at http://www.kaptest.com

<u>Peterson's</u> also offers Test Prep for the GRE, LSAT, GMAT, and MCAT at: https://www.petersons.com/graduate-schools/graduate-school-test-prep.aspx

<u>Peterson's Practice GRE test prep</u> Peterson's offers practice tests at this site: https://www.petersons.com/graduate-schools/gre-practice-test.aspx

<u>Princeton Review</u> The Princeton Review provides tutoring and assistance with graduate entrance exam tests, including the GRE, LSAT, GMAT, and MCAT. http://www.princetonreview.com/

<u>Veritas Test Prep</u> Another good choice for test prep is Veritas at: http://www.veritasprep.com

TOEFL

The Test of English as a Foreign Language for international students. http://www.ets.org/toefl

GRADUATE PROGRAMS AND ADMISSION STRATEGIES

Ph.D. Programs Online is a useful resource for students interested in doctoral programs, but there is limited information available about the organization. Nonetheless, in addition to their own blog (not updated very often, but found at http://www.phdprogramsonline.org) they include a comprehensive directory of blogs for and about graduate students and studies at http://www.phdprogramsonline.org/top-50-blogs-every-graduate-student-should-read.html.

PhDs.org is Similar to PhD Programs Online (above), and is a useful resource for selecting top ranked Ph.D. programs or getting a better sense of how a program you are interested in is ranked. http://www.phds.org/

GradSchools.com provides articles and advice on selecting graduate schools, applying, writing the personal essay and other useful information. It is a part of a marketing company called Education Dynamics which promotes online education, so there is a heavy focus on online programs. Moreover, it appears to be primarily marketing to international students (who pay the highest tuition rates). If you are an international student, their information may be more relevant to you, but even if you are not, the site may have some valuable information so is worth checking out. http://www.GradSchools.com

Peterson's provides information for prospective students, parents of students and educators about colleges and universities, rankings, graduate programs, demographics and degrees. Another commercial site, it does at least provide some helpful direction. http://www.petersons.com/graduate-schools.aspx

US News and World Report College Rankings Probably the most popular of college rankings, but not necessarily the most accurate, the *US News and World Report* rankings are at the very least something you should take a look at in making your university choices. www.usnews.com/rankings

FUNDING

Scholarships.com This commercial site provides an online searchable database of scholarships, but in order to use it, you must provide your name, date of birth, zip code and email address. It may be useful, but I'd be cautious of any website that wants that much information about you, particularly when it is a commercial site. Proceed with caution. http://www.scholarships.com

College Scholarships.org Unlike Scholarships.com, this site does not ask for any information of users, you can select the types of scholarships you are interested in, it provides helpful articles on writing the entrance essay and other tips and they even offer scholarships of their own, including $10,000 for students who maintain their own blog. This is well worth your time, but don't stop here; be sure to contact a grants librarian as discussed in Chapter Twelve. http://www.collegescholarships.org

College Financial Aid Advice This is a site that parents set up to help navigate the complex world of figuring out how to pay for college. It has an extensive listing of scholarships and grants, including corporate grants that you may not know about, as well as information on the application process. http://www.college-financial-aid-advice.com

MISCELLANEOUS

Grad Resources is a non-profit organization that provides e-mentoring, seminars, workshops and a crisis line for students who feel isolated or alienated in graduate school. They are less concerned with admission to graduate school than coping once you are in, but they are a refreshing alternative to the profit-driven grad resources out there that are heavily focused on internet educations. http://www.gradresources.org

The Council of Graduate Schools is a national organization that serves the interests of graduate schools and deans. It is less useful to graduate students, but gives you an idea of the directions, concerns and needs of graduate schools. http://www.cgsnet.org

<u>The Chronicle of Higher Education</u> The Chronicle of Higher Education is published for professors and university administrators. It can provide useful information on a particular school you are interested (or not, depending on whether they've written anything about the school), as well as topics of concern to academics. http://www.chronicle.com

<u>Inside Higher Education</u> Inside Higher Ed, like The Chronicle of Higher Ed, is another publication for academics and university administrators that may be worth checking out. http://www.insidehighered.com

ABOUT THE AUTHOR

Janice Harper received her M.A. in cultural anthropology from Western Washington University and her Ph.D. in anthropology from Michigan State University. She is a Fulbright Scholar and recipient of numerous fellowships, including from the National Science Foundation, Ford Foundation, and many others. She was a professor of anthropology for ten years at the University of Houston and the University of Tennessee before leaving the academic profession for a career in writing. Her work has appeared in *Psychology Today* and *Huffington Post* where she has been a regular contributor. In addition to her own work, she has ghostwritten seven memoirs and non-fiction books and hundreds of graduate admission essays.

Dr. Harper's forthcoming book, *How to Survive Grad School, Even if You're Overwhelmed, Burned Out, Or Have an Advisor Who Won't Give You the Time of Day (Unless You're Naked)* will be released in 2016. If you would like to be notified of its release, Dr. Harper can be reached at harper@janice-harper.com.

And please, do leave feedback on Amazon!

Made in the USA
Lexington, KY
07 December 2017